Many Lives
Intertwined

Many Lives Intertwined

a memoir
by Hyun Sook Han

with Kari Ruth

Introduction by Madonna King

Yeong & Yeong Book Company
St. Paul, Minnesota

Yeong & Yeong Book Company
1368 Michelle Drive
St. Paul, Minnesota

© 2004 by Hyun Sook Han

Cover and Interior Design by Kim Dalros
www.dalrosdesign.com

Library of Congress Cataloging-in-Publication Data on file with
the publisher.

ISBN 0-9638472-9-5

First Edition

08 07 06 05 04
7 6 5 4 3 2 1

Visit our website: www.yeongandyeong.com.

This book is printed on acid-free paper.

Printed in Canada

*For that reason, telling stories was as much a torment to him as an
attempt at self-liberation. He was at once saving himself, in some way,
and mercilessly, destroying himself.*
—W.G. Sebald, *The Emigrants*

Dedication

To all adoptive parents of adopted young adults,
children, and babies born in Korea, and to
Children's Home Society & Family Services,
with all my prayers, gratitude, love, and admiration.

Table of Contents

Mrs. Hyun Sook Han—what a remarkable, delightful, resourceful and courageous human being! For the nearly eight years I have known her, my appreciation and admiration for her life has deepened and intensified. I love Mrs. Han's child-like ability to sincerely laugh, cry, and be angry, playful, serious and irritated sometimes within moments of each other.

Shortly after coming to this wonderful agency in 1996, I began to study the history of the Korean people. I read book after book, my spirit filled with amazement and awe for what the Korean people endured, survived and triumphantly overcame, particularly since the first part of the 20th century.

During this same period of time I came to know Mrs. Han, a gifted individual born at a pivotal time and place in history. I have heard from her all of the accounts you will read here in *Many Lives Intertwined* and often think about how different her life was from mine.

Mrs. Han vividly describes having to flee from Seoul during the Korean War wearing a thick, quilted winter *hanbok* at age 11. What a contrast to my childhood! Mind you I was not a privileged child. I was raised in a large, lower middle class family and not without my share of responsibilities around the house. However, I was wearing peddle pushers and slacks, and I trotted off to the Catholic school I attended wearing my blue school jumper. My winters consisted of sleighing and ice skating; summers were filled with going to the swimming pool each day—all in the playful company of my three brothers and three sisters. While ours was not a family of financial resources, I cannot recall a time in my childhood when I was hungry, cold, or felt my security threatened.

Mrs. Han's life, on the other hand, included Japan's occupation of her homeland, during which time she was not allowed to speak her native Korean and was given the name

Toyota—"A car, imagine that," in the words of Mrs. Han. She came of age under the strong influences of Confucianism's social order, with filial piety being held up as the strongest and most important of social relationships. Confucianism is a very ordered way of living in which the male is always at the top of the structure—father, brother, husband, ruler.

Prior to the war, Mrs. Han enjoyed a childhood security filled with the established practices of a traditional Korean heritage. Her daily life was filled with customs, rituals, food and societal expectations that were followed for thousands of years. There was a certain rhythm and refuge in a society of this nature.

I cannot separate my view of Mrs. Han from this time when the fabric of Korean society was ripped to shreds. All that was comforting was taken away. Mrs. Han lost her childhood at a very young age when she needed to quickly take on a very responsible, protective role within her family. Imagine a small child having to carry her heavy sister on her back for hundreds of miles during a time of such turmoil. Imagine the shrill sounds of the airplanes and the bombs exploding, seeing the blood, hearing the human cries. Imagine having to go out in a strange and terrifying place to gather firewood for cooking and heat. Imagine seeing and doing things that no child should ever have to see or be responsible for doing. This is the backdrop of our beloved Mrs. Han's life.

Mrs. Han's experience in occupied and war-torn Korea was exceptional due to the many forces that came together simultaneously at a time when she was at such a young and impressionable age. First, her experience had a life-long impact upon every fiber of her being and provided her with the tremendous focus which is with her to this very day. Second, it was the fuel that drove the manner in which she chose to help piece back together this decimated society. Mrs. Han did not allow these harsh years to destroy her spirit; on the contrary, they inspired her to action.

It was that spirit that gave Mrs. Han the strength to resist her father's demand that she become a lawyer and instead pursue the education in social work that she chose as her way to begin to put the pieces back together for children. She broke all the norms. But she could also temper that strong will, as when she, in the manner of an obedient wife, followed her husband's wish to move to the United States. While that was our good fortune, it was not Mrs. Han's choice. She did it out of respect for her husband. However, even as she started a whole new life in America, she could not forget the lives she left behind: she remained very active in South Korea attending abandoned and vulnerable children and changing social policy for children. To this day, people in honorable places all over South Korea hold great respect for the indomitable Mrs. Han.

We all have such great respect for her. You will read in this book of the many lives she lived, framed by the Korean War and her move to the United States, and the incredible contributions she has made to international adoption. You will sense the tremendous impact she has had on a great many other lives, how she helped bring together families and children who needed each other, how she helped those same families later in their lives, as they dealt with issues of adoption and Korean heritage. She is an amazing woman, but before she tells her own story, let me share one anecdote of my own.

One of the great thrills of my professional career is to travel to South Korea with Mrs. Han and to escort babies to their families here in the States. Last December, three of us each escorted a child. Mrs. Han's charge was having a particularly difficult time. He cried and sometimes screamed for the entire trip and would not take fluids. We were all concerned about his well-being. Mrs. Han was so loving and patient with this little one. She walked him, rubbed his back, sang to him, and held him in the Korean style on her back. She was relentless in doing everything in her power to soothe this distraught baby. As I watched her amidst all the other sleeping passengers, I thought of the thousands of babies that Mrs. Han held in her arms, the diapers she changed, the bottles she prepared, the miles she walked comforting tearful children. Occasionally she would nod off for a few minutes to grab much-needed rest, as only Mrs. Han can. I saw a momentarily tired woman who selflessly gave her life's energy to others.

I sincerely congratulate Mrs. Han for the many different lives she has woven together and lived so well. She is now moving on to a new phase in her life. I am delighted that Mrs. Han will continue to dedicate some of herself to our mission by serving in a director capacity on our agency's Board of Governance. The world continues to be hers. Whatever she does going forward, I can assure you it will be with passion, dedication, focus and, most importantly, with a spiritual commitment to humankind.

We love you, Mrs. Han! Please take our love with you wherever you go.

Madonna W. King, M.A., L.H.D.
President & CEO
Children's Home Society & Family Services

Prologue

The day was January 4, 1951. Soldiers and police officers were going door-to-door, telling everyone to leave or they would be killed by the North Korean army. By Korean age, I was twelve years old. My sister was six or seven, my brother was five and my baby sister was three. Mother was weak from giving birth to my youngest sister just seven days before, and Grandmother was half-paralyzed; she could walk but didn't have use of her arm or hand on one side of her body. Father and Uncle had been evacuated by their company earlier and we were to wait for them at home. When the soldier knocked on our door, I realized that as the oldest child I was now the one in charge. I protested against the soldier's order, insisting that we had to wait for Father, but the soldier said no. We had no choice. We left.

I tied my newborn sister on Grandmother's back and carried my littlest sister on mine. There was no time to pack, not even food. We wore our regular everyday clothes, which included the traditional Korean socks. Everything was of the thickest cotton: my clothing and the blanket that tied my sister to my back. There was so much padding that my arms stuck out to the sides. I had difficulty walking, and with each step my little sister seemed to grow heavier and heavier, constantly sliding off my back. I had to stop and refasten the blanket every so often. But we kept walking, blindly, to the South.

By the next day, we were hungry and cold. A deep snow had fallen, which made our foot travels even more difficult. Another day passed and my newborn baby sister, too fragile for the weather and lacking food, died. I was relieved. I didn't care anymore. Starving, cold and exhausted, I wished my littlest sister, the one I carried on my back, would die too. All I could feel were my aching feet, sore back, pangs of hunger and chilled bones. I felt so tired as we walked day and night, I could not feel love. When we evacuated our home that day I learned how to hate, and I hated war.

The U.S. Air Force mistakenly dropped bombs on us, all of us refugees fleeing our homes, because the enemy was right behind us. The next morning, all I saw was bright red blood splattered against the pristine snow. Red and white. Dark and bright. So many bodies torn apart and so many children alive, their parents gone, and just as many parents alive, their children gone.

But we couldn't stop and mourn. We had to hurry. Snow bank to snow bank, thousands and thousands of us moved forward quickly and impatiently. More children were lost, left behind in the masses, or confused in the crowds. We walked all day and sometimes through the night. Snow bank to snow bank, I saw thousands and thousands of children, toddlers and babies, all of them crying, all of them left alone in the snow. They were abandoned in the night or separated from their parents in the crowds during the day. Sometimes, I slid my little sister off my back and set her down next to all the crying children, then walked away. But always, I came back. I was torn. I couldn't bear her on my back much longer and tried several times to abandon her, but for those few steps—my back straightened, the load lighter—I felt the heavier weight of family. No matter how fatigued I became, I could not leave her forever.

All those children crying though, I could not look into their eyes and acknowledge such sorrow. Instead, I whispered to them: "I will come back and help you. Somehow, I will find a way to help you."

At that young age, in a state of mental and physical shock, I didn't believe that those abandoned children in the snow banks I passed would die before I returned. I couldn't believe such a thing or I would have died too.

Growing up in Korea

My name is Hyun Sook Han. Before I was married, my name was Hyun Sook Shim. I should have been born a boy. That's what my grandfather dreamed: a grandson who would carry on the family name. My paternal grandfather was the first to know that my mother was pregnant.

"Have some meat," Grandfather said to his seventeen-year-old daughter-in-law. "I know it's your favorite."

"Thank you, Father," his daughter-in-law said. "I will have some later."

"No, no," Grandfather said. "You must eat now. Have more meat so your baby grows strong and healthy."

"What baby?"

Grandfather had dreamed about a willow tree filled with birds and leaves that reached high into the sky, then suddenly sprouted flowers. He said the flowers covered the entire tree, as well as a light. When he woke up, he knew this was the sign of a baby coming, specifically a grandson. The next morning he asked his wife if his daughter-in-law was pregnant, but when his wife asked her, the daughter-in-law said no. Still, Grandfather cooked her favorite meats, certain of her pregnancy, and two or three months later, my mother announced that she was pregnant.

So Grandfather knew of my mother's pregnancy before anyone, even my mother, but he misinterpreted his dream. All he saw were male symbols: a tall, big tree with lights—the sun, he thought—all around. He forgot about the significance of the blooming flowers. Maybe his desire weakened his divining powers. Grandfather was a successful business owner during this time. He owned a big grocery store and more than ten houses, which were investment properties. Some of those houses were made of mud and stone, and that summer, when my mother became pregnant, three or four houses were lost in a flood, and eventually that caused Grandfather to lose his business. He became very depressed and worried about the future of his family. Because his son, my father, was not an out-of-the-ordinary son in his own family, Grandfather hoped for a brilliant grandson who would continue the family name.

I was born a girl and Grandfather went numb. He just sat, motionless, refusing even food for three days. My mother thought he wanted to die, so great was his disappointment. She remembered all his attentions on her during her pregnancy, and now he said nothing, did nothing and ate nothing, and for several months I was called "Baby Girl" because Grandfather had only picked out a boy's name for me.

Years later, I found out that my legal birth date was not my actual birth date. My legal birth date was declared as June 15, 1938, but my actual date of birth was February 3, 1939. The discrepancy is probably due to my grandfather. Because he had no name for me those first few months, he probably waited until he had one before going down to the district office and officially registering me. Not wanting to explain to the district officials why he waited so long after my actual birth to register me, he probably put down that June date (of the registration) as my birth date. The difference in years was confusion between the lunar and solar calendars. Grandfather said I was born "last year," which, according to the lunar calendar, was 1938. By the solar calendar, however, it was really 1939.

I only have one childhood memory of my maternal grandfather. Late at night, he liked to cook beef over the small pots on our heated *ondol* floor, and sometimes he would wake me up and give me a big piece of salted, cooked meat. That's how I came to like meat so much. Grandfather raised my mother the same way, which is why she loved meat, too, and even fainted a few times if she didn't eat enough meat. That's how I am now. Even though I have high cholesterol, I need to eat red meat every so often or I feel faint.

My memory of my paternal grandfather might also be my earliest memory. I was maybe two years old and was eating fish when a bone got stuck in my throat. I cried and cried because it was so very painful, and I remember that Grandfather carried me to the doctor. We didn't have cars back then, so he had to carry me a long distance, alongside a stream. In between my cries, I heard Grandfather's calm yet strong voice: "Hyun-sook-ah, don't worry. I'm taking you to a doctor and doctor will take of everything." I believed him, as only a child can, with all my heart.

For many years, I resented my paternal grandfather for his disappointment in me being born a girl, but after I had moved to America and was a grown adult with a family of my own, I remembered the meat and fishbone stories and understood that he did learn to love me, and I came to love him.

My great grandmother on my father's side was a great influence on me in academics. She wasn't a typical lady of her time. Rather than sit around talking and gossiping and acting prim and proper, she liked to read. She never received a formal education because girls didn't go to school then. But Great Grandma was determined, and she educated herself by listening outside the boys' classrooms and reading over their shoulders. I liked to imagine her sitting outside the school building, squatting in her dress with her ear against the thin makeshift wall and eyes widening as she absorbed all that knowledge, or peeking over a boy's shoulder so she could read a book. So curious she was. Eventually she taught herself the Chinese alphabet. I was about five years old when she taught me the Chinese characters. I just assumed that everyone else was taught in the same way by their great grandparents. When I started grade school, I found out that many of my friends didn't know the Chinese alphabet, either because their great grandparents were dead or did not know it. That's when I realized how smart Great Grandma was, and how special. Before I started school, I could read and write because of her. Those lessons weren't easy though, because Great Grandma believed that learning should just come naturally, that I should just pick it up simply from being exposed to it; she didn't think math or reading or writing was something that had to be learned. For her, it came easily; I struggled.

"Try again, Hyun-sook-ah," Great Grandma said.

"Sky-chun..." I said, pausing as my five-year-old memory failed me again.

"And?" Great Grandma prodded. Her big eyes held mine as if searching for the answer. She had a round face, and I always thought I looked like her, just not as pretty. Great Grandma had pink cheeks, and back then people said that if you have pink cheeks you will have a long life; she already was in her late eighties.

"Uh, land-uh-ji," I continued, squeezing my eyes shut in concentration. Great Grandma wanted me to learn one thousand characters. One thousand. I wondered if I would make it.

I think of Great Grandma as a sort of genius. She was so smart. I admired her for that and her strong belief in educating all of her grandchildren—even me, a girl—so that they would be smart in school. In her own way, I suppose, she was trying to continue the family name just as my grandfather hoped to do when he dreamed of a baby boy. Unfortunately, Great Grandma's smarts didn't travel very far or wide down the family tree. Her second son and his family became doctors and lawyers and professors, but her first son—my grandfather—did not inherit such good fortune. The second son got all the good genes.

Her husband, my great grandpa, died in his seventies before I was born, so I never knew him and I never knew Great Grandma as someone's wife. To me, she was just Great Grandma, the Smart One.

Great Grandma passed away at age 93, and her last few years were spent inside the house, lying on the floor. I think she developed what we now call Alzheimer's, or maybe it was a form of dementia. She took to sleeping on the floor right below a crawl space we used for storage because that corner was the warmest spot in the room. No longer able to administer lessons, she slept and slept, lying on her side. Above her in the storage space were valuables my parents kept safe, including some of the best honey from the countryside, harvested by farmers who worked for my father. There were no candies or sweets in those days for children like there are now, so honey was the only real "candy" for us, and knowing that jars of it sat in that storage space was more temptation than my siblings and I could bear. To reach up there, though, we needed a stool. Great Grandma, the sleeping lump on the floor, became our footstool. We stepped on her to reach the honey, and she never moved, never complained. I don't know if she was even awake or if she just didn't mind. We didn't mean to disrespect her; we were just being silly kids who wanted honey, and Great Grandma helped us. Maybe she felt that was the last thing she could do for us. Maybe that was her way of rewarding us for learning all her lessons.

Smart as she was, Great Grandma didn't have much tolerance for anyone she didn't consider her intellectual equal, and one of those people was my grandmother—her daughter-in-law. Grandma wasn't educated, and Great Grandma didn't respect her because of that fact. To me, though, Grandma wasn't just the ordinary woman Great Grandma thought her to be. Grandma had her own gift, one she passed on to me: the gift of telling stories.

Grandma was the one who I had the most love for because she raised me. My mother had to wash and clean and cook and care for an entire household—Father, his mother (Grandma) and seven small children—at a young age. She was only seventeen when she became pregnant with me; by the time she was in her thirties, she had a house full of children. I bonded more with Grandma than I did with my own mother because the only time my mother had for me was when she gave me some chores. There always seemed to be a newborn baby who needed her constant attention. One baby after another.

Grandma, the storyteller, was a thin, pretty woman who never needed more than two pairs of rubber Korean shoes a year because she was so light and delicate on her feet. She used to complain about my mother, who needed several pairs a year. Grandma believed that Mother wore out her shoes because she didn't walk like a lady. Maybe part of Grandma's disapproval of her daughter-in-law came from her own unhappiness. Although we all thought her to be very pretty,

Grandma didn't seem to think so because her husband didn't pay her any attention. Grandpa was a rather peculiar man. There wasn't a girlfriend on the side as many men had in those days; Grandpa just preferred solitude to the comforts of his own wife. No one in the family ever saw the two of them sleep together in the same room (he slept outside of the main room) and we all wondered how they ever produced two sons.

During the hardest times, Grandma was the one who paid attention to me. She was the one who carried me on her back, tiny as she was, so I wouldn't miss a day of school. She was always so proud of me, telling me that I was the best and the greatest. I remember when I was number one in my classroom; Grandma believed me to be number one in the entire school. Father wanted me to become a lawyer, but I was never as exceptionally bright as he had hoped. Grandma's belief in me, though, gave me the strength to believe in myself and my ability to achieve the highest of expectations, to become a leader or number one in my school. With her in my corner, I believed I could achieve anything I wanted to do. I think I was like Grandma in a lot of ways. She was not as brilliant as Great Grandma, but she had a good memory and that enabled her to tell me all those wonderful stories she stored in her head. Now I tell those same stories. I remember I looked up some of those stories in books and couldn't believe that the book stories were exactly as Grandma had told me. Exactly. She remembered them word for word.

Before the war we had a lot of farmland, and Grandma used to supervise the grains and honey because my father was so busy with his own job in Seoul. She walked, sometimes two days, to the fields and often took me with her. In fact, she never left my side after the tiger story.

Back then tigers sometimes came down from the
mountains and roamed the countryside. I was about four or
five years old then, and for some reason I woke up in the
middle of the night while we were staying at the farm.

"*Halmoni?*" I cried out. "Halmoni, where are you?"

Rubbing my eyes, I pushed aside the warmth of my heavy
cotton blanket and got up to look for Grandma. She wasn't in
the room or the main room, so I went outside to look for her,
remembering the path we took to walk to the fields.

"Hyunsook-ah!" Father shouted. "Hyunsook-ah!"

"Where are you, Hyun Sook?" Mother yelled into the
dark.

"Hyun Sook!" Grandma said, as if willing me to her
through her voice.

"Halmoni!" I kept calling and crying.

My family panicked when they realized I was walking
around outside; they thought a tiger might attack me.
Grandma always regretted that. Even though I usually slept
quite soundly, she worried that I might wake again in the
middle of the night, and from then on she stayed by my side
every night.

Not long before the Korean War, Grandma suffered a
stroke that left her partially paralyzed on her right side. She
still could walk but had no use of her upper right side.

Grandma passed away when I was in ninth grade, after
the war, and I couldn't eat or sleep for ten days, so deep was
my grief. I thought we could have saved her if she had gotten
better medical care. She only had a fever, nothing serious.
Even though the doctor came two or three times to the
house, I thought he could have done more. Grandma was in
her early sixties when she died, still so very young. After her
death, I dreamed about her sometimes, and when I did,

something bad always seemed to happen: I became sick or there was an accident of some kind. Although I always remembered her as the person who cared most for me, about eight years ago, when my husband passed away, I started to dream of him and understood that in my adult life he had become the person who loved me most. And I stopped dreaming about Grandma.

That separation from Grandma was so difficult for me, and even today, I feel sad for children who grow up without grandparents. In my work as a social worker, I always ask families I am interviewing who want to adopt if there are grandparents because my belief is this: parents cannot love without judgment because they are responsible for raising their children, which includes praise and reprimands. Their love is layered—complicated and complex. This does not mean parents do not love their children completely; they just have to be tough sometimes, too. Grandparents can offer love without layers because they are not responsible for the day-to-day upbringing of the child. A grandparent's love is the simplest of all. That is what I believe. That is what I experienced.

My maternal grandmother passed away when my mother was three, so my mother never really knew her own *omma*. Her father remarried, but the new wife was not the kindest to Mother. In Korea, children from a husband's previous marriage often are not considered part of the "new" family formed when the husband remarries. The new wife (or stepmother, as we call her in America) often wants to start a family of *her* own with her husband and forget that he ever had a past family: a wife and kids. I don't remember this "step" grandmother, only that I always sensed she was an angry person.

Because my mother's home life wasn't very pleasant, she spent a lot of time at Big Uncle's house. We referred to Big Uncle's house as "ninety-nine" because that's how many gates it had. I remember the house as an enormous palace in which I frequently got lost. When that happened, one of Big Uncle's ten servants had to guide me to the right room. I think Big Uncle was in politics; that's why he was so rich. This side of the family, Mother's, also was very good-looking. They had fair skin, high noses and big round eyes, like the ones so many young girls today want through surgery. Mother, though, wasn't considered to be beautiful back in her day. In fact, people called her "cow eyes" because they found her large round eyes to be very strange and not very Korean. Big eyes were not my mother's most unfortunate attribute, however; she was unlucky enough to have a large chest. When she had to wear her fancy *hanbok*, she would be in pain and short of breath because it would be wrapped so tightly to flatten her chest, as was the fashion then, and sometimes she would nearly faint from the constriction. Grandma (Mother's mother-in-law) disapproved of Mother's too-womanly figure, which made Mother even more self-conscious. Not until the 1980s did Mother finally feel comfortable, when she was able to hide her breasts (without binding them) in the fashion of the time: sweaters.

Knowing all this about my mother's childhood helped me as an adult to understand why she seemed so distant to me, why we never bonded as mother and daughter. She really never had a chance to be a child—a daughter—herself. Her birth mother died before she got to know her, and her stepmother wanted nothing to do with her. There were no strong female figures in her life to teach her about being a young woman, a young wife and a young mother.

Even though she was old enough to have a child physically, I've often wondered if she was ever ready emotionally.

I was born a fussy baby. Years later my family said that I cried a lot and that my cries were predictions of bad times ahead. The saying went something like: if a child cries all the time, and the explanation is not that she is simply a colicky baby, then something bad is going to happen in the family. Because I was born finicky, the belief was that my birth triggered bad happenings. That was a family's fate, according to most Koreans back then. Although my family did not blame me for their bad fortunes, they did believe that my cries predicted dire events. One man, however, cured me of my weeping ways.

For a while, we used to rent the upper level of the building we lived in to earn more money when my father's business was lagging. A Chinese man, Mr. Wong, rented that level and used it as his residence and business: a Chinese restaurant. One day, I might have been three or four years old, I ran into Mr. Wong in his restaurant. I remember that he spoke a very broken Korean, and that made him sound even scarier to me.

"Ah, you are Hyun Sook," he said, "the one who cries all the time."

I looked up at him and frowned.

"Do you know you cry too much?" Mr. Wong said. "You make my ears hurt."

Tears started to form in the corner of my eyes and I scrunched up my face to hold them back.

Mr. Wong leaned down into my face. "If I hear you crying again, I will take you away from your family," he said. "Do you understand?"

He never heard me cry again. I didn't stop crying completely, but I made sure I never cried around him or my parents. For a long time after that, I was too scared to eat in his restaurant—until college. That's how scared I was of him. Mr. Wong should not have threatened me and ever since then, I made a vow to myself to never threaten a small child like that.

Father was the breadwinner and caretaker of our family. He was the one who gave me and my brothers and sisters baths every night, every single one of us, until I was about six years old. He also bought all of our clothes because Mother didn't know how to shop in the open market and haggle with the merchants. Her job was to stay at home and take care of the house and the children, so she never learned how to get along in the outside world doing the kinds of tasks we now take for granted, like shopping. I grew up learning how to do all of the same domestic chores she did and everything in between. Because my father had to work outside of the home, I was the one who took my siblings everywhere. If someone needed to see the doctor, I carried him or her on my back and supervised the visit. Father took care of Mother if she got sick. Without him, she would have died a long time ago because she wasn't very good at taking care of herself. He took care of her as if she were a little child. She acted fragile, and he handled her with the greatest of care, but that was my father's nature. He was overprotective of his children, too. In fact, my younger brother—the oldest son— never learned how to swim because Father refused to let him go near water so he wouldn't drown. When he was old enough to drive, Father let him take the test but never let him drive, afraid that his oldest son might die in a car accident. Can you believe that? So overprotective. And I have become just like him.

Great expectations. That was my father. He was a classy man: fastidious and always properly dressed up. Unlike my mother and I, he never spoke crudely or out of turn; he always considered his words before opening his mouth. His one downfall was his inability to trust anyone, and because of that, I sometimes became too trusting of all the wrong people and sometimes distrustful of the right ones, like my own family. If something went missing in the house, I would question my whole family. Of course, I always regretted my suspicions later. That is what I've inherited from my father.

Because his own father didn't think much of him, I suppose my father developed high expectations of himself and his family to try and win that approval. He never felt like he could be Number One because he lacked a formal education. I suppose that's why he coached me so hard to be the best. He wanted me to be what he was not.

Before I was old enough to start school, Father dreamed that I would become a lawyer. The problem was that my speech was slow. I wasn't dumb, but for some reason, my verbal skills took a while to catch up with my age. For a while, I couldn't speak. I understood what people said to me but I couldn't respond properly. All that came out of my mouth was, "Uh, uhhhh." Can you believe it? My tongue was just tied; nobody knew why. My parents didn't believe that I was mentally underdeveloped; they knew I was smart. I just couldn't get my tongue to work. My father insisted, though, that I practice speaking because he believed I had to be a good orator to be a good lawyer. So every night after dinner he made me stand up in front of Great Grandma, Grandmother, Uncle, Mother and all of my siblings and bow

21

and deliver a short speech. I think I was five or six when this started. When my speech didn't improve from this nightly exercise, Father somehow got it into his head that Christians were good speakers because they talked a lot. We weren't Christians then and had never been to church, but Father insisted that I start attending. Alone. This was my training, not his, and he felt perfectly justified in making me find my own church. He never expected me to convert.

I asked my friends in the neighborhood where to find a church and learned that there was one about two or three miles away. Back then, many of the churches were built into the mountains. There were no paved roads up those steep hills, and when I began attending it was winter time. I had a hard time getting up the hill, so I learned to wait for the adults to pass by and then lightly grab hold of their skirts or coats for support. The church ladies had no idea I was holding onto them. For many, many months after that I dreamed that I was walking up that hill but never reached the church.

In time, I learned to love church. I had an excellent memory and absorbed everything the teacher taught me. For my studies, I was rewarded with pencils and notebooks and such, which made me feel rich. Back then, few families could afford to buy new school supplies. I studied hard and learned the lessons, and still my father never came with me. That wasn't unusual, though. Many children attended church without their parents because the parents sent the children to learn and study but didn't feel a need to go themselves. To the parents, church was not about religion but about lessons they believed their children should learn. I suppose the church also helped alleviate some of the burden for feeding the children and providing them with small necessities, like my pencils. Children like me also earned extra gifts by bringing our friends or neighbor children, which I did often.

Funny thing is, my father said I didn't have to go to church anymore when I was in high school because I had become an excellent speaker. But by then I had come to love the church even though my father never intended for me to become a Christian. In fact, he did not approve of my decision to attend church. He only sent me there to improve my speech by talking with the well-versed Christians; never did he think I would become one.

Growing up in Korea meant living with hunger. Korea was still under Japanese rule when I was born. Not until 1945, when I started school (a couple months late, as my father waited for the Japanese occupation to officially end) were we free as Korean people. During the occupation, the Japanese exploited our country's rich agricultural economy by exporting large quantities of rice to Japan, causing a food shortage in our homeland. They also forced us to give up our mother tongue and speak only Japanese in school, and take Japanese names. This went on for nearly forty years. When the Japanese were finally defeated in World War II, and Korea was an independent nation once again, the country continued to struggle. We still had a food shortage, and because of it, many Koreans starved to death, including my childhood friend who lived next door. I remember knocking on her door one day to see if she could play, and her mother told me she had died. We were only six or seven years old. I was lucky because my family had some food, but I didn't understand this. All I knew was that my parents told me not to share our food with anyone because we barely had enough for ourselves. There was nothing I could do to help my friend, so when I heard her cry out from hunger, I could only watch as she hungrily licked soy sauce diluted with water off her fingers.

During the Second World War, the Japanese took what they could get their hands on. They took all of our good brass cookware and turned the metal into bullets. My Grandma dug holes in the floor of our kitchen in which to hide some of the special dishes we used for ancestor worship. We lost our chopsticks and bowls and rice cups, but those were not as important to her. So we used bamboo chopsticks instead of the silver or copper ones you see today.

In 1945, about July, my father came home from work and said that the Japanese had been defeated, and they now had to leave Korea. He worried that, in anger, the Japanese would try to shoot all the Koreans before giving up their decades-long colonial rule. Father insisted that we evacuate to the countryside. That day was very hot and humid—the middle of summer—and the countryside was as far as forty-five miles away. There was no motor transportation, so we were expected to walk all that way. My mother's relatives lived there, and we stayed with them for a couple of weeks until my father decided that Korea was totally independent and free of Japanese rule. When we returned home, we discovered that all of our neighbors were alive and well, and no one had left.

I am the oldest child. Before the Korean War, there were four of us children: three girls and one boy. During the war, one newborn baby girl died one day after the evacuation started, and premature twin boys died two days after birth when we returned to Seoul. My mother gave birth to three more children after the war so that we once again became a brood of seven.

In my childhood, my mother and I never really bonded; that came slowly in later years. She did bond easily with my youngest siblings. Maybe because she was older and more experienced as a mother; that knowledge gave her confidence and allowed her to relax and simply be a mother.

My brother, the oldest son but third child, is now fifty-eight. He was always a good son. Even now, as an adult, he does what my parents ask of him, no matter what the request. I never knew such a man. However, there was one time he went against our parents' wishes: when he married. My parents didn't approve of his wife even when they were dating, and the family resented the marriage because they did not feel that his wife-to-be was of the same social class, and they could find a wife for him. While they were dating, we tried to match him with another girl but the date never worked out. My brother refused to date or marry any other girl. Can you believe it? That was the only time he defied my parents.

"Mother, Father," I said. "Please let Brother marry that girl."

"Never," Mother said.

"She is not our kind," Father said. "She comes from a different social background."

"Yes, yes, I understand," I said. "But if you don't let him marry her, don't you see that he will refuse to marry anyone else?"

In the end, my brother married the girl that his family did not choose for him. She knew we did not like her and did not approve of their marriage, but my brother would not let her speak against his parents. He continued to visit our parents every week alone, for nearly twenty years. His wife refused to join him. She thought of us as the enemy. Only large family gatherings, like holidays, did she come along. Otherwise, she did not like to spend time with us because she felt as if we were judging her. I suppose we did, early on, but once my brother married her, she became family whether we wanted or not. What we didn't tell her was that, over time, we came to accept her as family. Sure, we still thought her beneath us in a way; that is the Korean way of thinking, but we didn't mean to sit around and complain about her or judge her unfairly. We had our opinions. She didn't have to agree. We would have liked it if she came to visit more often with my brother. Maybe we would have gotten to know her better and she would have gotten to know us. None of that seemed to bother my brother. He continued his weekly visits, always bringing fruit or some gift, and he supported my parents financially. My parents were very proud of him. Whenever he came to the house, the neighbors would say to my parents, "Oh, the good son is coming!" Even Father, who never really felt he had a remarkable son (I was Father's favorite), finally admitted in his seventies that he was blessed with a good son. Only once did he declare that in his lifetime, and I suppose that was enough.

The second child, my sister, is four years younger than me. She was always much prettier than me and also quite bright, even though no one realized this until much later. In college, she finally became Number One of her class. When that happened, she told me, "I became Number One! Do you know I always felt inferior to you because you were always Number One and a leader? Now I am." I suppose that is how it is with an older sister and a younger one. We were competitive. I think she's the smartest of all my siblings, but she's also very different. Nowadays, she's the one who gives most of the financial support to our parents, even though she's not rich. She lives in Texas in an apartment with her husband, and she's the one who stays with our parents now when they are in Korea. Unlike me, she can stay with them for one or two months.

Her husband is retired and she never worked, but they do well because they saved their money. I give away a lot of my money to friends or people who need it more than I do. My family thinks I give away too much. When I buy things, I end up giving them away as gifts. For example, I go to Korea and buy fifty purses in Itaewon and give them all away as gifts and my own purse is old and falling apart, like my shoes. My sister buys two-hundred-dollar shoes and a seven-hundred-dollar purse. I tell her, "Are you crazy?" She says, "This is my hobby." I say, "Hobby? It's just a purse!" And here's me, wearing worn-out faded blue slippers when I need summer shoes. Then again, I only buy necessary clothing. My Korean friends buy expensive name-brand clothes; I shop very, very cheap at TJ Maxx. Clothes and purses and expensive things are not my hobby.

This sister has one daughter. She didn't want any more children than that. In fact, she wanted to adopt a child but her husband said no. He wanted her to give birth, and if she wasn't going to, then he said they would have no more children. That is the Korean mindset; it is hard for them to want to adopt because family bloodlines are important. Luckily for my sister, her daughter had two children so she has grandchildren.

My other sister, the fourth child (third daughter), could be considered the prettiest one, but she is the only one of us who didn't go to college. She has two daughters now. Originally, she only wanted one child, probably because she was disappointed that the first was a girl, but we sisters pushed her to have another. After another girl was born, she and her husband decided not to have any more children, no matter what I said. Even today, Korean attitudes toward baby girls are similar to when I was born and disappointed my grandfather by being a girl. However, he came to love me; my sister also loves her daughters. In fact, her daughters are very beautiful like her. The oldest daughter looks like a model and the second daughter works for Korean Airlines as a flight attendant, and everyone knows that Korean Air only hires the tallest, prettiest and best English-speaking young women. I think both of the daughters are about five-feet, eight-inches tall. Their father is tall; my sister is my height: five-feet, one-inch.

Both daughters also married good-looking men, and each of them has a child. My sister takes care of both grandchildren so her daughters can work. She is the happiest grandparent. Even though she never gave birth to a son, she is happy to have two beautiful daughters, two beautiful grandchildren and two sons-in-law who are as close to her as they are to their own parents. In fact, they are like sons to her. Financially, my sister lives a difficult life and part of that, I feel, is my fault. After I had moved to America, I encouraged her and her husband to come. They did, but in less than two years they lost everything and had to return to Korea. Still, I think my sister is rich because she has such a good family life.

My younger sister, the fourth daughter, lives in Los Angeles with her husband. She was born after the Korean War. She has no children, but she was a schoolteacher and took care of her students as if they were her own children. She's like that with all her nieces and nephews, too. In fact, she often financially funds the high school education of her nieces and nephews who still reside in Korea (she did not need to support my children). She doesn't have to help her American nieces and nephews because high school here is essentially free. In Korea, parents spend a lot of money on extra lessons for their children so that they can excel and do their best on the college entrance exams. If students in Korea don't do well on those exams, their future is more limited than it would be in America.

Because this sister has no children of her own, she is the one who cries at the thought of losing our parents. She loves them deeply. Out of all of us siblings, she is the best Christian and keeps our family together. She calls me every week; I talk to her more than I do my own daughter. Sister also sends me gift money for all the special days and holidays. She now has a small dental lab and is a perfectionist who does beautiful work.

My other brother, the younger son, lives in Dallas, Texas. He now has one son and one daughter, but before he met his wife, he was the one who made several trips back to Korea to try and find a mate. Koreans use a matchmaker and have "meetings," which would be the equivalent of blind dates in America, I suppose. The man and woman meeting do know about each other beforehand, though; maybe it's more like being set up by one's relatives or friends in America. It was expensive to do this, as he had to buy plane tickets, so I told my brother not to keep going back because he was going to run out of money. He kept trying, and finally he found the woman who now is his wife. She is very pretty: thin, tall and a nice person.

I think he is the brightest, most outgoing and best-looking of all of us siblings. When he was six or seven years old, I was a college girl, coming home in the early evening when it was getting dark. About seven or eight little boys were loudly discussing something, and it sounded interesting. I stopped at the corner of the alley to listen, but they didn't see me. They were talking about who or what they were most afraid of. One boy said "policemen," and another said "tigers," and the last one said "the president." Finally my brother said "my big sister." All the other boys laughed at him, yet he was very serious. He continued, "You all do not know her; she is very nice to me, but if I'm really bad or naughty, she takes the belt out of my pants and hits my legs. It really, really hurts!" Then the other boys stopped laughing. All the boys were nice to me and never treated my younger brother badly, as they remembered what he said.

Today, he works at a computer company and runs a small business on the side. His children are learning to be very good students. My brother reminds me of my father in that respect. Education is very important to both of them.

Finally, there is my youngest sister. She lives only two miles from me with her three sons. We are very close, even though our ages are far apart. I could almost be her mother, age-wise. She was five years old when I got married and had my daughter. I am glad, though, that she is close to my daughter; they are like siblings. Because Mother was so old when she had my sister, my sister thinks of me as her mother figure, in a way. I feel the same way. She always helps me. When I have guests, she cooks for me. My husband, before he died, even expressed his appreciation for her. He said, "I do not think I showed great love for her and I feel guilty. She seems so sad to lose me." That was his tribute to her. While he was sick, she came every day with flowers and cried and cried. She is so hard-working and such a wonderful parent; she is the best, I believe. She also cares for the elderly here, probably because she wasn't old enough to do anything for our parents in Korea when we were growing up. Everyone has nothing but praise for her. I admire her caring spirit.

School Years

I was seven, maybe seven-and-a-half years old when I started first grade. When Korea became independent, my father held me back a couple of extra months so I could start my education as a free Korean who did not have to speak Japanese or use my Japanese name in school. I did have a Japanese name but I never had to register it. My Korean name is my official, registered name, Hyun Sook Shim.

My school was about three miles from my house, so it took me almost two hours to walk one way. I left my house very early in the morning, often before the sun came up, and I never missed a single day. Sometimes, when I was sick, I still insisted on going to school so my grandma had to carry me on her back all the way there.

I did well in grade school. I became chairperson and student president. Back then in Korea, the president had to be chosen by the entire school. My father was very proud of me.

So many of my teachers were memorable, but I especially remember a few. My first-grade teacher was a married man, and I wasn't used to being around older men who were strangers, so that felt odd to me. Families had to pay tuition back then, but I didn't know this, being a child. All I knew was that my father always gave me an envelope to give to my teacher, and I saw the other students do the same. My father told me the envelope contained a letter; I didn't know it was money. I have a picture with this teacher. We took a class picture, and I remember he asked me to sit on his lap. I didn't like that so I have a frown on my face in the photograph. That's probably one of my worst pictures in a long history of bad pictures. I think the youngest photo of me was taken when I was about five years old. I had very thin hair then so my parents had it shaved so it looked thicker. Unfortunately, the haircut made me look only worse, and I cried when we took our family picture. When I entered school I had to get my hair cut according to school regulation, which was no more than one centimeter up on the ear. I looked terrible. My hair was always a problem, but I was born with thin hair and still have it today.

The Korean War broke out when I was in fifth grade, so I definitely remember that teacher. We called her Old Miss because she never married. After the war, so many young men had died, so many young women never found husbands, and everyone called them Old Miss. Our Old Miss had pimples. And beautiful hands. Oh, her hands were so pretty. They were fair-skinned and each knuckle had the softest of dimples. I loved to watch her hands as she played the pump organ. She was a young lady, maybe only seventeen or eighteen years old. She was shy but very determined. I remember how she used to teach us music but she had a terrible voice. That didn't matter to her. She wanted us to learn how to sing and appreciate music, so we followed her cues, which wasn't easy because her voice was so bad.

What I remember most about her, though, was that she said no to me sometimes. I don't remember specific incidents, only that I was not used to being denied my wishes. Back then, I was a good student and often got my way in the classroom, even if I was behaving inappropriately (which I never thought I did). All I ever heard was yes. So when this teacher told me no—on more than one occasion—I knew she was as strong-willed as I, and I had to respect her for that.

My best friend in grade-school lived about a mile away. She saved my baby brother. This was in 1948 or so; my brother was three years old. We were in the midst of kimchi season and everybody spent the days in the fields picking cabbage. The work was hard and exhausting, so no one was watching my baby brother very closely. He was the only son at this time—the jewel of the family. As we worked, he must have wandered off on his own. By the time we realized, he had been missing for a while. We put down everything as soon as we realized what had happened and began looking for him. I cried and cried because he was the first son, the only boy—the boy I should have been—and I couldn't bear the thought of losing him and what that would mean to my parents. As dusk came, I saw my best friend walk up the path to our house—with my little brother in tow. Grandma shouted and screamed and cried when she saw him. We all ran out to meet them.

"What?" we said. "How did you find him? Where was he?"

"I heard a child crying outside of our house," my friend said. "So I went outside to see who it was and saw that it was your baby brother."

We couldn't believe how far he had walked, maybe more than a mile and a half. My parents were grateful to my friend for bringing him back. They brought a large bag of gifts to her home, and bowed for her help. Their annual gift to her continued for the next fifteen years. To this day, they pay her the greatest of respect. It was because my parents acted in this way that I learned similar attitudes.

By seventh or eighth grade, I spent more time in the streets than in the classroom. The war had ended and the armistice was about to be signed. We Koreans didn't agree with the truce. No one wanted a divided Korea; we wanted to remain whole. The students took to the streets and demonstrated and rioted. We wanted our voices to be heard, so we left our textbooks in our classrooms and walked the streets under the hot sun all day. Our dark hair and that hot sun was a bad combination.

Back then, students also had to stand outside every morning and listen to a morning speech from the principal. If it was cold or snowing or raining, we still had to line up, stand perfectly straight and listen carefully. I had become anemic due to malnourishment during the war, so I often fainted.

In grade school, there was a neighbor boy who was a friend of mine. He was one year younger than me, but a classmate, and a pretty-looking boy—not good-looking, but pretty. He was a good student, too, and I suppose his looks and smarts made him the target of bullies. One particular group of boys always picked on him. Because I was older and he lived in my neighborhood, I felt I had to protect him, and I did. Years later, when I was in my late thirties, I heard through mutual friends that he told everyone I was his girlfriend. He was married then and had a wife. They had seen me when I was on television for work, and he told his wife that I used to have a crush on him and that I was a very pretty girl. When I heard that, I laughed. I wasn't pretty, and while I liked him as a friend, I mostly thought of him as a little brother I had to protect. He misunderstood it as love. Boys are funny.

That's what I remember about grade school. Because of the war they were hard years, but there were good times.

To enter high school, we had to take a test. I was a good student so I wasn't worried too much about it and believed that my scores would get me into the best high school. My father thought so too. Father came with me on test day and waited. I felt confident as I took the test, and when I came out to meet my father I was smiling.

"I think I did well, Father," I said, then handing him my test papers. "The test was easy for me, but there was no math!"

Father arched his eyebrows but then his face fell and he looked ready to faint.

"Aiissh," he said and held up the last page. "Look!"

To my surprise, I saw a blank page. In my haste and overconfidence, I had taken the test without checking the back of the last page. I had missed the entire mathematics section of the test, and it was too late to do anything about it. I could not retake the test.

My high school was not number one—maybe number two or three—but my school was well-known for teaching etiquette, and in that area we were number one. Many people said I went to a "fancy" school that catered to children who were not necessarily the brightest but were some of the richest. We called them "downtown rich." Back then, the poor lived in the suburbs, and that's where I came from. I had to walk an hour to catch the bus, which I rode for only ten minutes, then got off and walked another thirty minutes. During those years, my legs became thick because I had to become such a fast walker. Still, I was late nine times. That was embarrassing, especially because I had perfect attendance. I wanted to be on time, too, but I lived too far away. As a result, I wasn't qualified to be an honors student but the teachers knew I came from far away so they made me an honor student anyway.

Our school, as I said, was known for etiquette, and we had a special etiquette center. Teachers from other high schools came to our school to learn how to teach. Of course, all of us students had to take etiquette courses. Unfortunately for me, that wasn't my area of excellence. My group got kicked out. I was strong-willed and stubborn, and so were my friends. That wasn't a good combination for behaving in etiquette classes. The principal eventually divided us into separate groups so we could at least graduate from the class. I was considered a strong and determined president of the student body back then. I was hard-headed and hard to control—all ingredients for a strong leader. My principal probably lost a few hairs over me, yet she loved me and remembered me into her late years.

We wore school uniforms then, and I remember that our school was the only one to have matching caps. My friends and I picked them out, and we were very proud to make our school stand out. However, I was embarrassed by my own homemade uniform. Most of the other students had their uniforms custom-made by a tailor, but we were too poor, so my mother found a wool blanket and made my winter uniform from that. The blanket wasn't new and had holes in it, so I ended up with a big mended spot where there had been a hole in the shoulder of my uniform. I was so ashamed of that. I would try to stand at a certain angle so people wouldn't notice it. In the end, though, no one paid attention to my shabby clothes because I was such a good student.

My strongest supporter was my tenth grade teacher. She taught home economics. Later, she became a college professor. Being strong-willed, sometimes I got into arguments with other teachers, but Mrs. Park always stood up for me. She really understood me and knew that I meant no harm. To other teachers, I seemed to have an attitude, and I suppose I did. If a teacher said something I knew was wrong, I corrected her. That embarrassed some of my teachers. I was a top student, but also a bit of a know-it-all, so some teachers didn't like me, like my geography teacher. I corrected her once and backed up my answer with the correct source, but she was very angry with me for embarrassing her. She was as strong-willed as I was. A very distinguished lady, she later became the principal of a highly respected school. I suppose, we were rather alike personality-wise, so we didn't get along; she really didn't like me. Before her, I had a male geography teacher and I liked him very much. He was not as distinguished and he was very poor, but he invited me to his home; even his wife liked me (I was the classmate of her younger sister). He wore glasses, never made jokes, and had a monotone voice while teaching. I took naps during most of his classes for a long time because, at the time, I thought that people with glasses can't see very much, especially details like whether I was awake or asleep. In my whole class of 65 girls, only one girl wore glasses. Later I found out that he mentioned my napping to his family, because his wife's younger sister asked me why I was taking naps in his class. I was truly embarrassed, so I started to pay much more attention, became the most knowledgeable student in the class, and came to like him. There wasn't anything particular this teacher said to me or did for me that made me like him; we simply got along well. Maybe my personality works better with male teachers.

Eventually, I came to like my female geography teacher; she definitely was memorable. Only a few years ago she came to talk to me at the hotel where I was staying with the summer Korean tour group, to discuss some personal issues about her family. I was sad to learn that she passed away a year or so later. That was a few years ago, but I am still very sad about her.

Unlike in America, Korean teachers command a lot of respect and students must obey them. If I challenged my teachers, I was showing disrespect by Korean standards.

Students were not supposed to question their teachers; teachers were always right. I had a hard time keeping my mouth shut though, when I knew they were teaching us the wrong lesson. Every so often, a student—like me—would speak up. I remember one incident in particular. We were learning English. Back then, our teachers were Korean and never studied English overseas; they learned it from other Koreans in Korea so they often didn't know they were pronouncing English words incorrectly. That day, we were learning the word, "hi." We had to repeat the word after our teacher, but our teacher was pronouncing it wrong. He pronounced it, "hee." Can you believe it? So there we were repeating, "hee," even though all the students knew it was wrong. Finally, one of the girls, a year younger than me, spoke up.

"Teacher Lee, I don't think we're saying it right," she said. "I think it's pronounced like 'high' not 'hee.'"

"What?" Teacher Lee said.

"I think we should be saying, 'hi,'" the girl said again.

Teacher Lee glared at her. "No," he said. "If I say it is 'hee' then it is 'hee.'"

The student persisted. "Teacher, if we say 'hee' outside of the classroom, everyone will laugh at our school," she said.

Our teacher thought a moment then said, "Okay, fine. We will all say 'hi.'"

His pride outside of our small classroom—among his peers—was more important to him than saving face in front of his young students. That day we were lucky to win the battle.

I loved my high school, my teachers, my friends and my activities. I will always remember the wonderful time I had.

The university exams were important in high school. We had to do well on them in order to get into one of the top colleges. If a student did poorly on the exam, that meant she couldn't get into a good school, and that later meant she could not get a good job.

Since I was a child, my father dreamed that I would become a lawyer. Lawyers had prestige and were paid well, and a woman lawyer would be very famous, as there was only one female lawyer in Korea at that time. That's why he sent me to church to improve my speaking skills. In high school, he made sure to remind me to speak slowly so people would listen and respect what I had to say. (Of course, it was too late by then. I already spoke way too fast.) For a while, I shared my father's dream because I believed lawyers helped the poor. As the university exams neared I did more research, and discovered that lawyers often prosecute the poor. They also had to memorize all the laws and read a lot of books. I was not good at memorization; that was my weak point. I also discovered that lawyers sit a lot, arguing their cases, and although I loved to talk, I did not like to do it sitting still. Ah, but my father raised me to be a lawyer ever since I was five years old. How could I disappoint him by telling him that being a lawyer just wasn't my type of job?

When I had to fill out application forms for college, I remembered my promise. During the war, I had passed abandoned children crying in the snow banks, separated from their parents as we evacuated, and I had made a promise to them to come back and help. Of course later I learned they had all died, but I still felt obligated to help other children. That's what I believed I had to do, so I asked around and discovered that I still had a chance to make good on my promise. I could go into social work.

After researching all the universities, I discovered that Ewha University was the only one that had a social work department. Just recently they had created the department. Before, social work fell under Christian education. Now social work was its own separate department, and I had the opportunity to join the first class of social work students.

"Father," I said, holding my chin high and firm, "I am going to Ewha to study social work."

"What?" Father said.

"I am going to study social work," I said. "I do not want to be a lawyer."

Father sputtered. "B-b-but, that is for poor people," he said. "Dumb students with bad grades go there because they can't get into the top schools. You just want to be an orphanage director?" He looked miserable, betrayed and disappointed.

My head lowered, I said, "I'm sorry Father. This is something I must do."

Father was sick. His dreams of me becoming a lawyer dissolved before him, and for years he never said much about me or my studies to his friends. Had I been studying to become a lawyer, he would have bragged and boasted me up and down, all over town. That I chose Ewha University *and* social work was an embarrassment to him, one he didn't get over until my junior year in college when I became student president of eight thousand students—the first student president from the Social Work Department, and elected by a vote of all the students in all the departments. Only then was he able to open up and brag.

My teachers were just as disappointed. They also thought I could do better, especially with my good language skills, but I persisted. I was going to study social work, and

I was going to do it at Ewha, a school that was not considered tops back then. My teachers said, "Why Ewha? You can walk into that school and graduate without studying at all."

Because I had disappointed my father and my teachers, I felt even more compelled to succeed and prove them wrong, but mostly I suppose I needed to prove to myself that I had made the right choice.

I entered Ewha University in 1958 and graduated in 1962. During that time, the school's reputation had nothing to do with academics; instead, it was noted for being the school young girls attended to groom themselves for marriage. Many of the girls had long, manicured nails and some wore silk blouses. All of us carried parasols because it was not fashionable back then to be suntanned. Fair skin and high heels were in. Over the years, I did my best to change our reputation.

In my first year, I became class representative; in my sophomore year I became vice president of the student body in the College of Liberal Arts and Sciences. Unlike in American schools, these positions had great meaning in Korea. To be the leader of your class was very important and highly respected, and it was the highest honor and source of pride for a student. I had reason to be very proud. Around this time, the Korean government was changed (post-war) and we had recently elected a new president, President Rhee, as a result of the Student April Revolution. I observed these changes and decided the same could be done on the university level. Up until then, class leaders were appointed, not elected. When I became president of the liberal arts college, I changed the process to a democratic vote. From then on we had elections.

When I later became student president, not just of my college but of the entire university, I continued my march of progress. I made changes and improvements, or at least what I believed to be improvements. One year, I rounded up all eight thousand students to purchase Flowers of Sharon, our national flower, and sell them to friends and family to raise money for post-war efforts. We collected enough money to purchase one navy surveillance ship to protect our east coast from another North Korean invasion.

Tired of our less-than-serious reputation, I did away with the parasols. At that time, all the girls were competing to buy the prettiest parasol and I thought that was a waste. Instead, I pushed to raise money to build libraries for countries that had no books for their students. I organized a group of students to perform for the soldiers stationed at the demilitarized zone (DMZ), and in this way show our support for those defending our country. That year was the first I was not an honors student because I was so busy.

Eventually, others came to recognize Ewha University as a good school. The prime minister came to campus and invited me to visit with him. I suppose I could have become a politician, but I never forgot my promise to those abandoned children: I would become a social worker. And I continued to disappoint my parents, who saw what a leader I had become and my other chances for prestigious careers, but I turned them down for what they probably believed was a silly promise. In fact, many of the young men and women who were student body presidents later went on to become government ministers and members of Congress.

So many people helped shape me during those years. The dean of students was one of those people. She cared for me when I was too busy to take care of myself. In her office, she always hosted a sort of potluck for some students. Sometimes I missed my classes because I was so busy organizing, and that meant I would miss lunch. If I didn't show up, the dean of students would seek me out and make sure I came by her office for some lunch. I really loved her for that. She cared so much for me.

Professor Reverend Han taught Christian education. I only took one semester from him and only because it was required, so I didn't think I was a memorable student. I simply attended his class. About five or six years ago, I was visiting the school as a special guest speaker. I was invited to a special dinner with the school president and some professors, and Reverend Han was there. Turning to him at the table, I said, "Reverend Han, you may not remember me but I remember you. I took your class many years ago." He looked at me and smiled and said, "Mrs. Shim (my maiden name), who does not remember you? Every professor remembers you." Frowning, I said, "Is that bad?" He laughed and said, "No, no, no. You were a very well-known student for good reasons." We both laughed then. The dean of the College of Liberal Arts and Sciences, Mr. Lee, used to say the same thing: "Hyun Sook Shim was the most memorable student president we ever had." He became a famous critic of Korean literature, so his kind words meant a lot to me.

Among my other supporters during college were Professor Lee, the social work professor, and Professor Choi—now Kim, by marriage. Professor Lee always defended me and recommended me for jobs. I have not forgotten her; she was my mentor then. Later, when I was hiring social workers she would recommend good students and I never hesitated to hire them. Professor Choi taught Human Growth and Development; she was at Ewha for only a few years. She is one of the brightest and most practical people I know, and a caring professor. We still keep in touch. Her husband was a dean at Seoul University and now they live in America. I loved her because she never spoke to her students like children. She respected us as individuals. Years later she met my husband, and he was impressed by her as well.

When I was a junior, Ewha University hired a new president, Dr. Ok Gil Kim. She was strict and not very personable, so I was a bit distant. Before her was President Dr. Helen Kim, whom I greatly admired and loved. Even though I worked mostly with the students and deans, she made an impression on me and I suppose I made one on her. Maybe ten or fifteen years ago I was in Korea for my work and I received a message from the now elderly Dr. Kim to come and visit her at her home. I was twenty-two when I graduated, and those college years seemed miles away as I listened to her message at age forty-five. She was dying, which I knew because I had read about it in the newspapers. Even though I loved and admired her, I hadn't planned on visiting. She was part of my past, and I was a person who always looked forward, but I couldn't ignore her message. I called her back, with my heart pounding.

"Hyun Sook, come see me," Dr. Kim said.

"When?" I asked, hiding my guilt for not having called her first. All this time I knew about her declining health and never bothered to visit her or call.

"Tomorrow at lunchtime," she said.

"I have nothing to bring you," I said. Korean manners dictated that I bring her a nice gift, but at the time I was a social worker with little money.

"I don't need anything," Dr. Kim said. "Just come."

I canceled my appointments and went there empty-handed and filled with dread. Can you believe that? I felt awful but I had no choice. This was the least I could do.

Dr. Kim's house was behind the school, and everyone knew that she never locked her doors. She had a beautiful flower garden along the long path to her door, and I wanted to linger with the flowers rather than face the person inside. When she opened the door, I saw that she had become small and thin. She grabbed both of my hands in greeting, and I bowed a traditional Korean bow; the formality made her laugh. "Look at Hyun Sook!" she cried. "A grown woman bowing!" In my awkwardness, I had broken the ice. Inside, I saw that she had guests: the president from another university, many professors and her younger brother, Professor Kim. My embarrassment rose again, and I bowed to everyone.

She told me that she asked her cook to make a special lunch just for me because I was visiting from America. We were served many traditional Korean dishes — so many good things.

"So Hyun Sook, tell me what you are doing in America," Dr. Kim said.

I told her about my social work. Since I had seen her, I had made good on my promise to those abandoned children I passed during the war evacuation. I was now working in Korean adoptions, finding orphaned Korean children homes in America.

"I am so proud of you, Hyun Sook," Dr. Kim said. "I have seen you many times on TV here. Now, do you know why I asked you here?"

I nodded my head no.

"I need your help," she said.

She went on to tell me about a letter she received from a Korean professor living in California who had a daughter and son-in-law who wanted to adopt a Korean child. The problem was that no agencies in California did Korean adoptions, so they wrote Dr. Kim for help.

"I remembered you," Dr. Kim said. "I remembered that you were working in adoption. We need your help."

"But Dr. Kim, my agency does not do placements in California, either," I said. "I do not know if I can help, but I am indebted to you, so I will try my best." And I did. The adoption was approved, and later my agency went on to do ten more placements in California.

When our discussion was over, we continued to eat and Dr. Kim gave me a half bowl of her rice as a gesture of her love. Even though I was full I ate it, because I knew she was happy watching me eat. "You have a good appetite," she said proudly. Before I left, she gave me money. I could not say no because it wasn't polite, but I couldn't bear to use the money on myself. Later, I heard that there was a Methodist missionary group in Sierra Leone that needed money to fix a schoolhouse roof so the students could study. I sent the money there on behalf of Dr. Kim.

Three months after I returned to America after that trip, Dr. Kim passed away. I wished I had gotten to know her better when I was a student while she was president. She did teach me a lesson I still try to practice today. Three things, actually, she taught me: first, rejoice always; second, pray continuously; and third, always give thanks. These were lessons I had actually heard most of my Christian life, but I never followed them until I heard them from her because I saw that she lived her life according to these principles. She was an example, and I tried to model my life after hers.

Some of my best years were my school years. I loved school so much and worked myself so hard, but those beloved school years are done and I can't go back. That's how I am. When I am focused, I give one-hundred-and-twenty percent but once I am finished with that part of my life, I do not look back. I cannot. All I can do is look forward and move on to the next stage.

Korean War

The movie *Snow White* was in the theaters when the Korean War broke out. I was in fifth grade and our entire school took a field trip to see the movie. All of us students were so excited and didn't mind the three-to-four-mile walk into town. At the theater we sat on benches; there weren't individual seats back then. With the benches, a theater could pack in hundreds of people. There were several soldiers in the theater as well that Saturday; they were on leave for the weekend and had come to enjoy the movie.

We must interrupt the movie to make an important announcement. Would all soldiers please return to their stations immediately. I repeat, all soldiers return to your stations immediately!

"Shut up and turn the movie back on!" a soldier shouted.

"Yeah!" yelled another. "Show the movie!"

"We want to see the movie!" someone shouted.

Please! All soldiers, you are ordered to return to your stations immediately!

"Snow White! Snow White!" they yelled.

There were boos and jeers from the soldiers, who wanted to stay through the end of the movie. They were so naïve, but then how could they know what was about to happen to their country and their people? We were only school students, fifth graders; we didn't know anything except that at that moment we didn't like the soldiers. Because of them, the announcement came on ten, maybe twenty more times, interrupting the entire screening until the soldiers finally gave in and left.

And war began.

June 25, 1950. I was in fifth grade. All of a sudden I saw this stream of people, many with children in hand, teeming into the streets of Seoul.

"What's happening," I asked.

"The North has attacked at the DMZ!" someone said. "We are coming from the North before it is too late."

I stared. All my school years, I had been taught that Communists were bad; we called them "Reds." I imagined red bulls with horns. However, this lady was a North Korean but she was not red. She was a human being.

At home we listened to the radio reports. The announcer kept telling us that Seoul was secure, we were safe, our armies were fighting back successfully and the situation was contained. That's what we were told, so we stayed put. Over the radio waves, our government assured us of our safety and our victory; evacuation was unnecessary, they said. None of us knew that the next day, June 26, President Syngman Rhee and his cabinet fled Seoul for Taejon, well south of Seoul.

Two or three nights later, bullets zipped back and forth over our heads. Father told us to head for the mountains; there were caves we could hide in. Mother, Grandma, my siblings and I left our house and made our way to the mountains. We used a stone bridge as cover along the way as the bullets whizzed by us. I remember thinking they looked like little sparks. Creeping like army infantrymen, we noticed that many South Korean soldiers were going deeper into the mountains like us, and we asked where they were going. Some of them had left their troops; maybe they were separated from their units during the fighting. I remember one young man who was maybe nineteen or twenty. He told us, "I'm going to use this grenade on myself but not now, not while you people are here."

The next morning we were hungry. We didn't have time to pack before we left, so we had nothing to eat. My little brother was picking up leaves off the ground and chewing them.

"Yah! Don't eat!" Grandma shouted at him.

"Why? I'm hungry, Halmoni," my brother whined.

"You eat, you get diarrhea," Grandma warned.

My brother kept chewing; he didn't care. He cried and cried, "I'm so hungry."

Eventually, the sounds of gunfire dissipated and we headed back down the mountain. Once in the main street, we saw that it was filled with dead bodies. The bodies were in the middle of the street and to the side of it. Those in the middle had been run over by the North Korean army tanks. The ones on the side seemed to have been moved there; there were no covers over their faces. All those young men in Korean Army uniforms, their eyes open. I mistook them for being alive.

"Ma! Ma! They're alive!" I yelled.

Mother shook her head. "No, don't bother. They are all dead, Hyun Sook."

Until that moment, I never knew that people died with their eyes wide open. I never saw so many dead bodies. Thankfully, I couldn't smell the stench—or maybe I don't remember. All I remember is feeling a sickness inside, wanting to believe that they were alive, not wanting to think that they had to watch their own deaths. These young men were not just soldiers; they were somebody's father, son or brother. One of them could have been my own father, my own brother.

On June 28, the South Korean army blew up the Han River Bridge, severing the link to Seoul. Many of the South's own military, as well as civilians, were killed in the blast. By midnight, Seoul fell to North Korean forces.

For a while, we learned to walk among the Communist army. I remember being surprised that they looked just like us. They were Korean, not red bulls with horns. At first, they were kind to us. They let the adults go back to work and the children return to school. At school, they taught us their national anthem, and we learned that their music was more advanced than ours was in the South. I liked their music; it was exciting and encouraging and proud. I didn't understand fully what was happening; in my child's world, I was just learning new songs.

My parents, meanwhile, were planning an escape. Early on, the North Korean army asked for South Korean volunteers to join their ranks. My uncle, Father's younger brother, was one of those who volunteered. He came into the house after work one day and announced that he was going to join the North Korean army. He was only twenty-two or twenty-three. My father was furious and beat on his younger brother as if they were children. Father's brother ran away from home and never went back to work for the North Koreans, so he was saved. Once the North took hold of Seoul, they became impatient with the volunteer system and simply took South Korean men away. My father went into hiding.

For the three months that the North kept its strong grip on Seoul, my father was in a very cramped hiding place. When he finally was able to come out, he could barely walk. He hadn't had any exercise for three long months.

In the fall, we heard on the radio (that we kept hidden under blankets) that American troops had landed in Inchon and were nearing Seoul. They were almost here, but not yet. When the Communists heard this, they rounded up their men in the night and went house-to-house, killing all men and kidnapping prominent and famous South Koreans. We fled our house for a relative's house downtown. We walked, and I remember that was the first time I saw a different-looking person.

In Korea, no matter how hot the temperature, neither men nor women ever took off their tops in public, especially in 1950. I was walking down the road with my mother, Grandma and siblings when we saw our first white American soldiers. And they were bare-chested, with no shirts on. I remember the date, September 28, exactly three months after the Communist occupation of Seoul. The American soldiers had hairy bodies and faces. Busy fighting from ships stationed in Inchon, the soldiers hadn't bathed or shaved in days. That day, they were moving forward into Seoul, recapturing it for South Korea. I stared openly at their white skin and half-naked bodies.

"*Halmoni, Halmoni!* What are they?" I said as my eyes grew wider at the sight of each soldier. "They cannot be human beings."

Grandma nodded. "Yes, Hyun Sook, they are human beings."

"From where?" I asked.

"From Western countries," Grandma said confidently. She seemed to know all about these strange foreigners even though she never went to school or traveled abroad, and I wondered where she had learned about these Western countries, as she called them.

"*Halmoni*," I whispered. "They have hair just like monkeys."

Grandma said, "No, they are humans, but they are not civilized."

The street was filled with them: whites and blacks. Some of the whites had bright yellow hair, and some had dark suntanned skin; others had pink skin and red hair and still others had black skin and white eyeballs.

"*Halmoni!*" I shrieked. "There is a black color! And a red color! They are so different."

"*Ne*," Grandma said. "There are all kinds of human beings, and I assure you, Hyun Sook, these are human beings, only they are not civilized and that is why they are able to help us fight the war because they are strong, like gorillas."

To me and Grandma, these large men were like Vikings. We imagined them eating with oversized knives and forks, like giants. "I bet they eat with pitchforks!" We laughed at our clever joke. Ha, ha, ha. Just like the Vikings.

Years later, long after the war, my husband told me a story about the hairy American men. My husband was from the North and had escaped as war broke out, but he had heard that the North Korean government was telling its soldiers that even though the Americans were joining the war, they would not be a threat. North Koreans believed that the Americans were sending old men to fight. In wartime, who has time to shave, right? But in Korea, only grandfathers wore beards. Young men did not; it was not appropriate. So the North Koreans believed that these bearded men were old and would not have the energy to fight.

You see, most Koreans had never seen a white person before, so they seemed so strange to us. I remember the first time I saw a white American soldier who had bright blue eyes. "Aah!" I screamed and pointed. "He has blue eyes!" The young man looked at me and my friends, not understanding what we were saying, and not knowing that every time he looked at us with those buggy blue eyes he made us scream more. Never before had we seen such crazy eyes. We felt sorry for him because we thought his vision was impaired; we thought all he could see was the color blue.

By the end of 1950, South Korean refugees had fled their homes and headed south to Pusan and outer islands. Nearly half of Seoul's population (one million) had left by the end of December. We were next. This was to be my second evacuation.

In early January 1951, the Communists recaptured Seoul and we were forced to leave our home. The company my father and uncle worked for was evacuating its workers and ordered my father and uncle to leave Seoul. All of us should have left together, but my mother had just given birth to my baby sister and was too weak for such a journey. Grandma had also become half-paralyzed by this time (as well as hard of hearing) and could not use her right arm or hand. I was twelve (in Korean age); my younger sister was six or seven, our younger brother was five and the next youngest sister was three. We could not leave home, so father stocked up on food and firewood for us before he and Uncle left. "They will not kill women and children," he told us. "Stay here and wait for me to return."

On January 4, 1951, an officer of the army and a policeman came to every house and told everyone to get out. He said we would all be killed if we stayed. The oldest child of the family, I realized that I was the one left in charge. I argued, "We must wait for our father to return, sir." The soldier wouldn't listen; he insisted that we leave. Now. So I strapped my young sister on my back and put the newborn baby on Grandma's back, and we left home.

There was no time to pack (again), so we left with what we were wearing and that was our heavy winter traditional Korean clothing, which meant no pants, not even a more maneuverable skirt. With the heavy blanket used to secure my sister to me, I was so bundled up I could barely hold my arms down at my sides. Winter in Korea is like winter in Minnesota, and we fought cold and snow as we walked south, out of Seoul. As we walked, my sister kept sliding off my back and I had to refasten her repeatedly until I grew so weary and burdened by the extra uncomfortable weight that I imagined letting her slide off my back and leaving her behind in the deep snow.

We were the last of the refugees to evacuate Seoul that cold, snowy January day, and I remember it well because that day, and many more days to come, carved scars forever into my memory.

The next day my newborn baby sister died. The elements were too harsh for such a fragile human being, and all I could feel was relief. She was one less body to feed, one less load to carry, and in my joy at this realization, I wished that my other sister, the one I carried on my back, would die as well. Is that hard to believe, that I felt no guilt over the death of one sister and the wish for the death of another? I don't think it's unbelievable; I think it's understandable. Under that kind of stress, in the midst of such strange trauma, a person thinks unbelievable thoughts. A young girl in charge of her weak mother, sick grandmother, and too-young siblings wishes for death, because in death one no longer cares. Love is not a factor in the equation of war. No way. Had I allowed myself to feel, I would have died too, and no one would have been able to care for my family. That's why I understood all those parents who had abandoned their small children in the night and didn't seem to care. There was no time to care; the slightest bit of remorse would have killed them all. They had to go on, just as I had to—without regret, without tears, without looking back. There would be plenty of time for all that later. In those days, we simply had to survive.

The American soldiers were evacuating alongside us. Down the road we went: white American soldiers next to South Koreans. Those soldiers seemed so big to me because I was so little, just a child. Our own Korean army didn't have any trucks then, so the American troops were the only ones to be carried on wheels. The ones who walked moved much faster than the rest of us. To amuse myself, I tried to walk in the snow prints of a soldier. For every one of his strides, I had to take five. All day long, we moved, pushing and shoving our way through the crowds of other refugees, heading further south to what we hoped was safety. Every night I was so sleepy, but I could not sleep more than two or three minutes at a time. Our bed was the snow, and we huddled together, trying to sleep while sitting up. Overhead, U.S. airplanes dropped bombs on us by mistake, because we were so near the enemy. By morning, the snow had been steeped in a deep, deep red.

We hurried ahead again, snow bank to snow bank. There were thousands of us, but we seemed to be millions, millions marching in the deep red snow. I saw young children and toddlers and infants sitting in those snow banks, crying for their mamas and daddies and sisters and brothers. Try as I might, I couldn't tune them out. The crowds were so thick, some had gotten separated from their parents while others had been abandoned as they slept through the night. Their cries chilled the air and their faces broke my heart. I could not look at them. Hurriedly, like the others, I passed them by, trying hard not to look, not to hear their frustrated pleas. Every so often, in my own frustration, hunger and pain, I slid my own sister off my back and laid her down in a snow bank, then walked away. But I always came back. As much as I could not bear to carry her much longer, I knew I could not bear the heavier burden of my heart if I abandoned her. So I pushed forward and whispered a promise to the children crying out around me: I will come back to help you. I was twelve years old. How was I to know that all these children would be gone or dead by the time I returned?

Each night during the evacuation it was my responsibility to find a straw mat for my family to sleep on, and that was a difficult task as there were so few. I had to scrounge, just as I scrounged for water to make rice. I don't know how I provided for my family. At that time, I didn't even know how to make rice yet, but there I was, retrieving water or fresh snow to melt into water for rice. We were better off than some, though. Sewn in our clothing and blankets was money; we were able to buy some of the things we needed from others. Our distant relatives also helped us, like the night my brother almost froze to death. They put him on their backpack, out of the snow, and saved him that way. From them we also had six spoons and a small pot for rice. Our problem was finding rice to make in our small pot. As we passed towns and villages, we begged at every house. If the house was empty, we tore down the frame for firewood. No one felt bad; we did it as a group to survive. There were no shops with goods for sale; everyone had to make do with what was available to them. When we finally returned to our own home later, the same fate had visited us; our house had been torn down for firewood.

Finally, we settled in a town known for its hot springs. In fact, it had once been a popular honeymoon place. When the war began the American troops set up camp there, and when

Seoul was recaptured the town was again transformed into our new home: the hot springs refugee camp.

There were so many refugees, each family had a very tiny space to call its own. We had to sleep on top of each other to conserve space. My youngest sister suffered the most because she slept on the bottom and couldn't even cry out in pain or discomfort; she couldn't move, and was unable to stand up or walk. No matter how careful we were, she woke up every morning with swollen legs.

My life became even harder at the refugee camp. My mother fell into a sort of depression and sat immobile all day long. She had lost her baby and was without her husband; I think she lost her will to live. So it was my responsibility to care for her, Grandma and all of my siblings. Finding water with several thousand refugees congregated in one area was nearly impossible. We were given rice by the American troops, but they gave us American rice: the long-grain kind. I didn't know how to cook it at first and had to learn. Eventually, I figured out that I had to add more water.

The most difficult job I had was to find firewood. Because everyone was in such a concentrated area, all of the natural resources in the immediate vicinity were used up right away. Some days I had to walk as far as six miles to find a few sticks of wood. There were large trees closer to the camp but I had no tools to cut them down, so I had to pick up whatever I could find on the ground. I remember that there was a shortcut to one of the places that had some wood, but I had to cross a river. Afraid of heights, I couldn't bear to cross that bridge for wood that was probably rotten, as much of it was then. So I was always last back to the camp because I had to take the long way to find my wood. Sometimes on my way back I would nearly faint, because my hemoglobin was so

low. To this day, because of my malnourishment then, I still
have to watch my hemoglobin levels or I might faint.

Grandma knew of my fainting spells and that they were
due to malnourishment. She loved me and probably
understood that I needed to stay healthy so that I could
continue to provide for the family until we found my father.
One day, she and I went to the open market near the camp,
and do you know what? We used some of our money to buy
me sweet rice cakes. I don't know how many I ate; I didn't
care. I was starving and greedily shoved rice cake after rice
cake into my mouth, and felt it warm my starving, bloated
belly. Grandma didn't eat any, and when I had eaten enough,
I asked her if she wanted to get something. I didn't know we
had used up a lot of our money. Grandma only said, "No, I
am full." Happy, I returned to the camp, only feeling a pinch
of guilt over the fact that we did not bring back anything for
my sisters or brother or mother.

Life continued like this for the next eight or nine months,
until we finally found Father. I had sent out messages and
asked all over about Father. Where was he? He too sent
message after message inquiring about his wife and children,
and one day he simply showed up at the refugee camp.

"Hyun Sook?" father cried out.

I didn't move; I couldn't. All I did was stare at him, my
mouth wide and opened in the shape of an "o." Mother and
Grandma stared, too. No one said a word, no one cracked a
smile. We couldn't even cry. Up until that moment, I had not
realized that I was terribly tired. After that, my life became
better; I was once again a child.

Moving around so much, displaced from my home as a
child, I grew up having difficulty trusting people and letting
them get close to me. That's why I understand adoptees. Most

American grown-ups do not understand what happens to a child psychologically when she is moved around a lot, with no place to call home. Of course the child develops attachment problems and has nightmares or worries about a variety of things. Look at me. I'm sixty-five and still have fears of water and bridges and hunger and lost children. Such bad experiences sap one's strength. A person does not leave that behind without scars.

First, Father moved us out of the refugee camp to Kyung Sang Province, farther to the south, closer to Pusan—the countryside. I was a city girl before the war, so living in the country was a new experience for me. I started a new life there. Among the other students who had been educated in the country or at home, I was the one who had read the most books. Soon, I became known as Doctor Storyteller. Every night after dinner, all the girls in the village gathered up baked potatoes and ripe tomatoes from their kitchens and brought them to me as an offering in exchange for a story. "Tell us a story! Tell us a story!" they demanded. I loved to tell stories, so I had great fun. When we left that place, I felt bad that I could no longer share the wonder of stories with the girls.

By the fall of 1951, we had returned to our home in Seoul, or what was left of it. Like the homes we stripped for firewood as we evacuated, ours had met the same fate. Father went to work every day but his company could not pay him. Once again, we were starving. Every day we heard of a child's death in our neighborhood; everyone was starving.

I returned to the fifth grade and learned that our school had grown smaller. Before war broke out, my fifth-grade class alone contained eighty students. By mid-war, there were only about one hundred students total in the entire school, and I became student president of all of them.

There was one boy I knew before the evacuation who was in my same class after we returned. Before the evacuation, he was the class representative. I knew him because of that but we never really talked because he was a boy and I was a girl. Back then I thought he was fairly good-looking. During the evacuation I saw him pass by. I was carrying my sister on my back and was hungry and sleepy. The day I saw that boy was a day I was especially tired and frustrated that we could not rest longer, so I cried as I walked with my family. As soon as I saw my classmate, I stopped crying out of embarrassment. I didn't want him to see me crying like a baby girl. We didn't say anything to each other that day, and the next time we met was back in school after the evacuation. I was elected to be the chairperson of our class and he was relegated to vice-chair. Because he was a boy, I was sure he was sore about losing to a girl so I wrote him a letter.

Dear Classmate,

Please do not be mad at me. I like you very much so do not feel bad. You can talk to me about this if you want.

Signed,

Hyun Sook Shim

The next day our teacher announced to the class that she was aware of some inappropriate behavior going on between certain boys and girls in class. We all wondered what she was talking about. I had no idea she was referring to my letter to that boy. Do you know what that boy did? He showed my letter to all his friends, and one of the other boys in class brought my letter to the teacher. The whole class laughed at me. The teacher made it seem as though I had written that boy a love letter when all I did was try to make him feel better for being only vice-chair. I shouldn't have written I like you. Back then, that meant something else. My mistake. I hated all the boys in my class that day. After that, I was sure not to write any more letters like that to any boys.

Home life in Seoul after the evacuation didn't improve much because everyone was so poor and hungry. Mother came out of her depression as soon as Father returned, and she took over the chore of finding firewood. During this time she became pregnant again. We were happy and hoping for a boy so badly, but this wasn't a good time for her to be pregnant as we were malnourished. As a result, the baby was born premature—and the baby wasn't one, but two; she had had twins. Twin boys. Our wishes had come true. We were so, so happy, Father and Grandma, especially. I didn't understand that the twins were born too early (at seven months) and were as malnourished as Mother was. They died shortly after. No one told me what happened, only that the twins were so small they were being kept safe in a special secret place. I opened every cupboard, turned over every box and looked under all the pots for their secret place. When my parents saw what I was doing, they finally told me the truth. I cried all day long, not because I loved them but because I knew how much it meant to my father and mother to have had boys.

Around this same time, I was left home alone one day. Everyone had left for some reason. Our house was still in shambles. We had no front door; most of the good wood had been used for firewood. I was sitting out in front of our house that afternoon when a neighbor lady told me, "Hyun Sook, there's a place you can go if you have a little money, where you can buy food." I went back inside to get a pot, then went to look for this place.

The food being purchased turned out to be the leftovers from a nearby American army camp. All the leftovers were thrown out in a big drum that served as a garbage can, but someone, a Korean, saw an opportunity. He emptied the drum's contents, mixed all the leftovers together, boiled it and sold it to people like me who were starving. Problem was, none of us knew where the "stew" came from; we had no idea that we were buying garbage. With just a little money, I could fill my small pot with that stew. If you were lucky, your serving might include a piece of fat or meat or a bite of hot dog. There were even hot dog bun bits, and all of it was mixed in ketchup. That's what I remember most; the stew was almost all red. I picked out the toothpicks and non-edible bits; they didn't bother me much. In my hunger and greed, I ate the entire pan. There was nothing left to bring home to my family. I finished all of it myself, and I suppose, as punishment, it's no surprise that I passed out fifteen minutes later. Right before I fainted, I remember thinking that I couldn't breathe and couldn't sit comfortably. I thought I was dying, and that was my punishment for not sharing all that garbage food with my family. I don't know how many hours passed before my mother woke me up. "Open your eyes!" she said. Or that was what I told myself as I gained consciousness. Once I awoke, I was fine. That day I learned that overeating when you are starving is much worse than simply starving. I didn't know when to stop eating—and didn't care what I was eating—and so I had made myself sick.

My husband had a similar hunger story. Born in Pyongyang, North Korea, he was the only son in his family.

His older sister married a man who went south to become an army colonel in the psychology department for the South Korean army. Later, he returned to his hometown and wife in the North, but when the war broke out and the fighting pushed north, he was one of the first to leave for the South. This brother-in-law of my husband's came by the house of his wife's family and promised to return and pick all of them up and take them to safety in the South. They waited and waited and finally the last of the South Korean army came by on its way south. My husband's parents asked the officers about their son-in-law and were told that he had fled days ago and was not coming back. Desperate, my husband's parents pleaded with the officers. "Please, this is our only son," they said. "Please take him with you so that he may be safe. Our son-in-law is your colonel. Please take our son." The officers agreed but only had room in the truck for one passenger. My husband was fourteen. Later, his parents tried to escape but they were captured and had to remain in the North. By the time my husband finally was able to return to North Korea, as a grown American citizen, everyone from his immediate family, including his parents, already had died.

Once safe in the South, my husband—a young man then—had to support himself. At age sixteen he was more grown-up than most boys his age because he had been on his own for a few years, so he lied and said he was twenty-one so that he could become part of a special troop that took out Communist guerrillas. He did this not because he wanted to fight or be a war hero but because the army was the one place where he could get regular free meals. They assigned him to Cholla Province where there were many mountains; the Communist guerrillas had been hiding in them for years. Few people ventured into those remote mountains. My husband was scared to death. When he settled in with his troop, he discovered that his companions were starving, too; there was no food in the mountains. They had run out of supplies and had no substitutes, not even stale bread. On top of that, they couldn't have fires to cook or the guerrillas might find their location. They had rice but no water and no way to boil the water to cook the rice. So there was my husband, sixteen years old pretending to be twenty-one, fighting guerrillas on an empty stomach.

One day his group finally came down to a village to refill their supplies, and also to fill their empty stomachs. A few young fighters, about five, couldn't wait until the whole group's food was prepared. They ran to one of the last houses in the village and aimed their guns at the poor lady of the house. They told her to cook rice and soup as soon as possible. The rest of them sat down outside while my husband watched the poor woman. As soon as the rice and soup and kimchi were ready, he quickly ate his fill, because he was very hungry. When he rejoined the men outside of the old house with the food, everyone immediately dug in, not knowing that my husband had already eaten his share. "Eat, eat!" they said. "Are you crazy?" My husband knew that if he said he had already eaten they would punish him, so he tried to shovel in a few handfuls more. By the time everyone finished, my husband was horribly sick to his stomach. Everyone jumped into the truck to head back to their post in the mountains, but my husband was too full and too sick to get into the truck. Normally, he could leap up into the back of it but that day he could barely get himself out of the kitchen of that old country farmhouse. "Get in, get in!" his comrades yelled. "What's wrong with you?" But all my husband could do was moan and hold his stomach. Finally, the others stopped the truck and pulled him in. That was when my husband confessed.

Years later my husband and I laughed and laughed about our starvation stories. Of course, they weren't funny then but we were able to laugh about them as adults. We carried the scars of those hungry periods into our adult lives, though. For me, I have to eat whenever I see food. I cannot fast because in the back of my mind, I think that if I do not eat I will starve. This is also why my heart breaks every time I think of the starving, orphaned children in Korea. My husband's starvation as a young man lasted longer than mine. After he left his mountain troop, he still had a few coins left from his military duty so he came to Seoul. With the last of his money, he bought a piece of bread—poor man's bread. The next week he starved. Many years later, in America, after he died in 1995, I went into his closet to throw out his old clothing. Do you know what? I found money in every single pocket of every piece of clothing. I think the total came to eight hundred dollars. Can you believe that? That was his scar of hunger and war. My husband believed, even as an adult in America, that he always had to have cash in his pockets and wallet or he would starve and die. He always carried at least one hundred dollars on him at all times, but often he forgot about it. I think he probably walked around with hundreds of dollars on him most of the time, between the money in his wallet and the money he had forgotten in his pockets.

Some fifteen years after the armistice was signed and peace was restored in the South, families began abandoning children. While many were abandoned during the war, many more were abandoned long after it because of the devastation of a war fought on our own soil. Our country was rubble;

post-war times were hard. Families could not afford more children, and because there was no such thing as birth control in Korea at the time, couples kept having babies. When the parents could no longer afford to feed the next child, they left their children somewhere—like a train station or in front of a hospital or at someone's door; a public place where the child would be found—and wished for them a better life.

I remember worrying about all those abandoned and lost children. In wartime, many of them were simply lost in the chaos of the evacuation. One minute a mother might be holding her daughter's hand, and the next minute, in the frenzy of a fleeing crowd, the mother would be standing there holding air. After the war, hundreds of thousands of children had been separated from their parents and it was difficult to help them look for their families. Back then, children called everyone by title, not by name, including their family members. If we asked the lost child where he lived, his reply was: *by my neighbor.* We asked him for his mother's name; he replied: *Omma.* How about your father? *Appa.* Brother? *I have two brothers—First Brother and Second Brother.* Even if we were able to find out a lost child's family name, there were too many other Kims and Parks. These children only knew their own names. They could describe their families, but every mother and father had black hair.

The government tried to help and started a campaign to reunite families separated during the war. Mind you, these were not North and South reunions; they were reunions among South Koreans who were separated. Some families were reunited this way, but many families were lost to each other forever. The children were put in orphanages and later adopted to other countries. If a family finally tracked down the lost child to an orphanage, often it was too late; they couldn't recognize their children unless there had been a birth mark, or perhaps their children were already taken by other Korean families. Some children ran away and were never heard from again.

During those post-war times, the streets were teeming with orphaned children. Even those of us with families were starving. Beggars filled the streets. Most of us ate someone else's leftover food. We didn't even have white rice then. We ate barley rice; it tasted awful. To this day, I cannot eat anything with barley or wheat, not even wheat bread.

Because most of us were ourselves starving and scrounging to feed our own families, we had nothing to offer all the orphaned children in the streets. Sometimes the street kids were able to bully us schoolchildren for whatever pocket change we had on us. I remember walking with friends in our school uniforms, white blouse and black skirt, and being surrounded by threatening kids with dirty little hands. If we didn't give them money or something, those street kids were ready to dirty our uniforms.

Before the war, nobody knew that orphanages existed. There were maybe three or four non-Catholic group homes according to government records, but these were not used by the greater public as orphanages; their existence was not known. By 1965, when people began abandoning babies, orphanages were part of the public vocabulary and the government began rounding up all of the street children and putting them into these homes. The big cities had as many as five thousand children, ages six to eighteen, in their orphanages around that time. At one time, it was estimated that there were as many as seventy thousand children spread out in three hundred and fifty orphanages.

Love

Marriage

Children

My father always told me: "Hyun Sook, you are going to be a very famous and successful person someday." I don't know why he thought that, because no one in our family had ever been famous, or even very successful. It was nice to hear that from him, but he didn't always leave it at that. In addition, he also insisted that there was one thing I had to be aware of, if I were to be a success: "Don't have a boyfriend, don't ever fall in love until your mother and I arrange your marriage, because we will find the most suitable person for you." As I have said, I never felt that I looked attractive or pretty. I said, "Don't worry, Father, I'll never do that." And so I never had any boyfriends when I was younger, even though my dream, when I was in junior high and high school, was that I always had somebody I loved. I always had one or two people whom I liked, but I never had dates or even exchanged sentiments like "I like you" or anything.

I always attended girls-only schools, even in college. I never had co-education, so there was no way I could have a romantic relationship with a boy. When I was a sophomore in college my friends all got good grades and were leaders in the school, and they didn't have boyfriends either. We decided that we should develop some kind of dating skills or we would never meet boys. Back then, girls didn't just ask out a boy and boys didn't take girls out on a solo date. We had what is now called a "meeting," in which an equal number of boys and an equal number of girls arrange to meet for a group activity. Really, it's like a group date. One of the girls in our group had a cousin in engineering at Seoul National University. She asked her cousin to get together some of his friends to match our group of seven girls. Because that would have been a rather large group, we ended up with a match of five boys to five girls. The five of us went to meet the five of them, but they were disappointed that we were not pretty girls! At the same time, we were disappointed that they were not good-looking boys. But there we all were, so we decided to just get together. At first we were going to meet once a month, but that didn't always work out. We met maybe five or six times per year. We went on picnics together, we met at the coffee houses, we had that sort of get-together. We ended up growing close, not as boyfriends and girlfriends, but more like brothers and sisters! In a way, that's what I wanted, because I did not have an older brother, and I didn't have any cousins who were boys, so it was nice to have friends who could give me advice like a brother would. We were all very close. I dearly miss them. After that time together, we all went on to have jobs and get married, and our relationships were over. For one thing, a Korean man (like my husband) would never, ever meet another man whom his wife knew a long time ago, even if he wasn't really a boyfriend.

While I was in college, at the all-girls school, every winter we went to the northeast side of the DMZ and visited the Korean soldiers and some American soldiers. I was vice president of the school body, and a sophomore at the time. We went there frequently for the next three years and developed good friendships with the soldiers, as well as with the professors who escorted us.

For our senior graduation party, my group—I was the leader, as always—said, "Let's get boys and girls together, the same number of each, and have a final party without any teachers." That's the first time we did that. I'm sure about one-quarter of the girls already had dates, including myself. A classmate's brothers graduated from the Army Academy, which is like West Point in America. They were three years older than us and they were already officers in the Army. These were eligible young men and they thought it was a great idea to have a match meeting. We just did it for fun, because many of us already had boyfriends. One of my classmates was followed by one of the officers everywhere she went. Her family was very upset with him, but he did it anyway. But now they are very happily married, and have three children.

I met my husband in my sophomore year. A few girls wanted to learn some English conversation abilities, because we didn't know how to develop our speaking skills. We could read and write English, but we never could speak it very well. But social workers had to be able to speak some English because the jobs required it. One of the girls knew a radio station announcer, a young soldier. His pronunciation was excellent. We decided to ask him to help us. There were five or six of us who agreed to pay him in exchange for a one-hour lesson each week. We were given use of an empty room in a beauty parlor for our lessons. (I remember the strong odor of perm solution that filled our small room.)

My husband-to-be was working during the day at that radio station in the U.N. Compound, and then he was going to college at night. He was a refugee from North Korea. He was a part-time driver. He was good looking and he was a very kind and polite man. All the girls liked him! He had left North Korea during the war as a young teenager, without his parents, so he was not the kind of fellow my parents would ever let me date. They never liked North Korean people because they thought that they were all Communists, or that they were a different kind of breed. One of the girls from that English group liked him and also wanted to tease him, so she set up a date with him that she didn't plan to have. That bothered me a lot, because I didn't want the men to think that we were all liars. She refused to go out with him that evening, even though I pushed her hard. So I went out to let him know that she couldn't make it, and ended up talking to him for a long time.

From then on, I started to like him, because his conversation and his manners were so different from the other young men we saw in our group. It went on for two years, and no one figured out that we were dating. Usually we went to see a movie and have dinner, but we never walked together on the street. He did everything for me. I loved Chinese food and we ate at Chinese restaurants a lot. After our wedding, he never wanted to go to a Chinese restaurant again. I asked why and he said, "Because I hate it!" I then asked why he ate there all those times. "Because you liked it." Many things were that way. For instance, I was always late for dates because I was the class president of the whole school, so I was busy with meetings. At that time there were no telephones or pagers, so he had to wait for three hours sometimes. And after we got married, if I was late by five minutes after he said, "Let's go out," then he would get angry. I said, "How could you change so much?" And he said, "I hated that you were late all the time." So now I've become very good about not being late, thanks to my husband.

I wondered about my husband's parents. I could not meet them, because they were in North Korea. He told me he was more like his mother in personality, and how much he looked like her and was more like her height. His father was a very, very tall, huge man and very loving and open-minded. His mother was from a very upper-class family home and was shy. My husband had both their traits—he could be open and show a lot of leadership, like his father at certain times, and at other times, he wouldn't want to do anything in a group, and he could be easily embarrassed by little things.

The funniest thing that happened when we were dating was one time when it snowed and was very slippery. In Seoul, we don't have snow or slippery conditions very often. If snow comes, it melts right away. But that time it didn't melt and things were very slippery. At that time, girls all wore high heels so he had to help me walk on the slippery sidewalks. I was holding my books because college students at that time didn't have backpacks and we all carried two or three books, whatever we needed for classes. Because it was so slippery with my shoes, he was holding my arm. But right in front of the Chosun Hotel, the most famous hotel in downtown at that time, with hundreds of people walking there—we both fell down! My books went everywhere and we were on the ground, and I wanted to die right there. But then we laughed, we laughed very hard. He was more embarrassed, I'm sure, than me. He was a man and was supposed to help me, but he fell also. So that was the funniest story.

We decided to get married, but when I told my parents they were shocked. They couldn't find any words. My father was very disappointed and tried to stop me. Even my pastor tried to stop me. My pastor asked me, "Are you pregnant?" I told him that I wasn't. He said, "Then don't marry. Just stay single longer." My pastor was very, very disappointed. Nonetheless, I still asked my pastor to officiate at the wedding. First he said yes, but when I brought our invitations, he said that he wouldn't. I asked why not. He said that he only did wedding ceremonies in a church, and I had planned mine for a wedding hall. He said he had never done a wedding at a wedding hall. So we argued back and forth, and finally I said, "Then I'm not going to get married!" "Good! That's what I want," he said. But then I cried and I begged his wife, so he did it. After that, he started doing weddings everywhere, not just in a church.

When we started our married life together, we were very, very poor. That was 1962, and Korea was in a deep and serious depression after the war. That depression continued until almost the middle of 1975, when I moved to the United States. Even though my husband and I both worked and earned good incomes, we couldn't buy very much. There just wasn't much merchandise in the shops.

Our life was very, very hard. Several months after we got married, I became pregnant with my daughter. The morning sickness went well beyond what I could handle. I threw up every single thing I ate. I lost weight and I couldn't sleep. I was too weak. I couldn't cook for my husband and I never cooked for myself either, so it was a hard time for about five months. My lowest weight was 95 pounds in my fifth month. My average was 100 to 105, and I felt like I was almost dying. But in my sixth month, I starting eating again and I became swollen. I began to put on weight quickly, so the doctor checked to see if there was a toxic condition. Everything was healthy and normal, but I had to eat a lot, because I was always hungry. I drank a lot of water and that also made me really big and swollen. At that time, we didn't have maternity clothing for pregnancy, and it was terrible because I couldn't wear my own clothes. I only could wear my husband's jackets or

Right: Mrs. Han in junior high, one of the few photos taken in her younger years

THE WHITE LIONS

Top: High school friends—best students and leaders in specific areas such as academics, talent, and looks; called themselves the White Lions because they were special. [Han standing, 2nd from left]

Bottom: Mrs. Han [left] with mother [center back] and two high school friends.

Top: *Sophomore year in college–Professor Lee in cap became Ph.D. in philosophy, the leader of the Social Work Department. [Han top row, 2nd from right]*

Above: *Freshman year in college–at grade school reunion. [Han front row, 4th from left]*

Freshman: *Junior in college; husband kept this photo in his wallet until he died.*

Top: *Junior or senior in college on a picnic with high school students. Han [front, center] was the leader of this church group.*

Above: *Freshman year college with two best friends. [Han, left]*

Right: *Sophomore year of college; emceeing one of several engagements and special events in Korea.*

Top: *The wedding: April 24, 1962; with friends.*

Above: *Wedding with both sides of the family [Mrs. Han's mother left of Mrs. Han; father above slightly left of Mrs. Han]*

Left: *Engagement photo, senior year in college.*

Left: Mr. Han, 19 or 20 years of age, looked more like 30 years of age at that time. He wanted to look older because he was job searching.

Above: Mr. Han receiving award with fellow employees of UN Radio—Best in Volleyball.

Right: Mr. Han [right] in his early 20s, with best friend.

Top: *Freshman year in college, Han [2nd from bottom] with Social Work Department friends.*

Bottom: *Sophomore year in college, vice president of student body for College of Liberal Arts and Sciences. These were all representatives of different parts of the student body. Dean of College of Liberal Arts [man, front row center] later said his most memorable student body president was Mrs. Han. [Han middle row, far right]*

Above: Senior year of college–tradition to take class trips. [Han front row, 3rd from left]

Above: College graduation 1962; [from left to right] with friend, future husband, mother and younger brother [6th brother].

Top: *Freshman year in college; group of high school English students who got together before their former teacher left for the United States. [Han front row, right; high school English teacher next to Han]*

Bottom: *Han vice president of student body at the time; went to the DMZ to entertain soldiers from United States of America with dancing, singing and comedy. Mrs. Han was English emcee. In the back row, men are deans and professors. [Han second row, 2nd from right]*

Above and Right:
Sophomore year in college—representatives of students from Social Work Department visiting Marine Corps. [Photo above: Han second row, 2nd from right; Photo right: Han standing, left]

Bottom Right:
Sophomore year in college; practiced English with group. [Han standing, center]

Top: *1966 at SWS for 5-6 months. [Han, far right]*

Bottom: *1964 ~ took this photo to send to Mr. Han when he was in Vietnam.*

Top: *Sophomore year in college; group of student leaders with the dean. [front center] [Han back row, far left]*

Bottom: *Junior year in college; entire social work class. [Han lower row, behind first row seated, center]*

Top and Below:
*At picnic during
sophomore year in college.*

Left: *Senior year in
college; Han [back row,
2nd from right],
president at the time,
with representatives of
student body and the
Dean of Students. [front
center]*

Top: 1968 ~
working at
International
Social Service,
attending meeting
of Korean and U.S.
agencies. [Han 2nd
from right]

Right:
Han [left] with
CAPOK adoption
staff member and
her two sons.

Top: *1971 - TCIP, arriving in the U.S. for training. [Han front row, 2nd from right]*

Left: *Going to TCIP, leaving for the U.S. at the airport. Han [in white] with Holt president [far left], daughter Shinhee [front], mother and father [next to Han, right and far right]*

Left and Below: *1969 ~ Han [center] received a government award from the Minister of Social Service. The award was received for great service for in-country adoptions.*

Bottom: *Mrs. Han spoke at this conference in 1974. She talked about unwed mothers; no one thought that junior high and high school girls could be pregnant. After her speech, she was invited to visit factories throughout the country and talk to young men and women. [Han third row, 5th from left]*

sweaters, that's the only size I could wear. And my body got so big, like a balloon.

Finally I got close to the time for delivery. The pain started two weeks before. My husband was afraid of that, and he put me into the hospital for three days, but nothing happened. The doctor sent me home. Then finally my water broke and I went back to the hospital. My mother came from home and waited until the baby was born. My daughter was almost 8 pounds, so she was a big baby for a Korean. My husband only called the hospital and checked. He just didn't want to come yet. The men usually didn't go to the hospital during the waiting period, or even for the delivery. That's why some mothers exchanged babies when they had daughters, because their husbands didn't know whether a boy or girl was born. After the delivery, that's when my husband came to see us.

It was a hard delivery. I was there for three nights and the pain only stayed the same and did not become faster. It was still the same, five minutes, five minutes. By the third night, I wanted to die because I was so sleepy and tired. When I finally delivered with some help from a machine, I bled too much and was unconscious for the next couple hours. They couldn't find my vein for a blood transfusion. I was in very serious condition. My mother said, "You shouldn't get pregnant again."

After all that, my husband was very disappointed. He had wanted a boy. He wanted a son, because he was the only son of his family. Plus he's from North Korea, so he wished he could have a son and show his parents at some future time, if he could ever go to North Korea. So I was disappointed too, that I did not give him a son.

We didn't have a name picked out yet. His family generational name was not appropriate for a daughter as an

ending name, so we decided to make up a name of our own.
I said, "How about Shinhee?" He said, "Fine." So that was
my daughter's name. It means "faith of hope." He agreed
with that. I was very pleased to have picked such an unusual
and wonderful name, and she still keeps that name.

Shinhee was a healthy and cute girl. She laughed from
the time she was one month old, even before that, she
laughed aloud. And then my husband said, "She laughs like
my father." His father laughed so loud, the whole
neighborhood knew where his father was, he said.

When my husband took Shinhee outside during the
summer, everybody complimented him, "Your son is very,
very healthy looking and very good looking." Then he would
say, "No, she's a girl." When she started to have hair, she
looked so cute and was clearly a pretty little girl.

After Shinhee, I didn't want to get pregnant again, but
knew that eventually I would want to have another child. I
was on birth control pills for the next seven or eight years.
When I was in my early or mid-thirties, I decided it was time
to have another child. I got pregnant, but miscarried. That
happened again and again. I miscarried six or seven times. I
cried and prayed and begged God to help me. During this
time I worked full time as a social worker, very hard, and it
never occurred to me to quit my job and stay home.

"Stop it, Hyun Sook," my husband said eventually. "You
are going to die. Let's adopt." I was surprised because
carrying on his bloodline was so important to him, but he
insisted. "I don't care," he said. "I don't want you miscarrying
all the time. You are going to die if you keep that up. We will
adopt."

"Are you kidding?" I said. "I am going to have another baby by giving birth."

"You won't be able to keep it," my husband said. He insisted that we adopt.

Finally I agreed, and we applied to the very agency where I was the director. It might be considered strange, because who was going to interview the boss, after all. But it was our only choice, because my agency was the only one in Korea doing in-country adoptions at that time. So I asked our three supervisors, "Hey, what do you think, who is going to interview me?" They all laughed and one supervisor said, "You love your daughter too much. I don't think you can love your adopted child the same way." And I believed her. So I told my husband what she had said, and he said, "Oh yes we will. Don't worry about it. We will love the new child the same as our daughter." But I said, "No, I have to be sure I could love the same way." It's hard to believe that I didn't understand how a mother loves her child no matter what, whether by birth or by adoption. In my years ahead, I would certainly see that in all my families. But my husband had already figured that out. Almost a year later, I finally said, "Okay, I want to do the home study."

The adoption supervisor selected the youngest social worker, who did not know me personally, just that I was her supervisor's boss. At that time, we didn't interview the prospective parents as a couple; the interview was done alone with each person. After the interviews and the paperwork, the young social worker came to our house for a home visit. Of course, she had to approve me!

We didn't want a newborn, because of my work schedule. So we said that we wanted a little boy, older than one, but not older than three. Many people thought we selected my son from among hundreds of boys. But that wasn't the case at all. Our agency was an in-country adoption agency, so whenever a baby is older than around seven or eight months, we couldn't find a family, because everybody wanted a newborn or a very young baby. We transferred those older children to the Holt Agency—we were in the same building—right away. My son's intake social worker told her boss, "I have a one-year-old boy. What should I do? Should I transfer him to Holt or do you have a family for this boy?" Her supervisor told her that I had asked for a child of that age, so she should discuss it with me.

We had been waiting for a boy of that age for several months and my husband was getting a little antsy. He asked, "How come you can't get a boy for us?" I called my husband and told him that our social worker would bring a baby boy to him. This particular social worker was one who counseled unwed mothers when they decided to make an adoption plan for their child. She would be the one who needed to find a foster home for the boy. I suggested that they could use us as a free temporary home instead of placing him in a foster home, where the agency would have to pay. Children stayed in foster homes until all the medical checks were done.

So they brought him to my house so that my husband could meet him. He cried at first, but then my husband held him. At the end of the visit, when the social worker wanted to take him back to the orphanage, he cried and grabbed my husband. So my husband said, "Just leave him." She came back to the office and told me that the boy did not want to leave my husband. When I got home, the little boy still clung to him, maybe because it was the first time he had been separated from his birth mother, and he needed someone else to hold him.

Our foster home social worker took the boy to the hospital and had all the tests done. They said he had several allergies and tested positive for lung tuberculosis. We had to give him a lot of medicine for his TB, which he cried about and resisted. After about a month of struggling with his medicines, my husband suggested that we just stop using them, and let him be cured naturally with good nutrition. Within two years he was cured, and no one else got TB from him.

We decided he was meant for us. We named him Shin Up, which means "faith is successful or accomplished."

My father telephoned me after the adoption. "What did you do?" he said. "How could you do that without telling us?"

"Father," I said. "When we decided to have our first child, we didn't ask you if we could become pregnant."

"This is different," he argued. "You bought an orphan!"

"We adopted, father," I said. "He's our son now."

Later, we called my father's older sister (his only other living relative) and told her the news. At first she only said, "Oh." Later, she reconsidered and decided that we made the right decision. Still, our family treated my daughter and son differently. Shinhee was almost eight at the time our son was adopted, and she was the most loved then because she was the first grandchild. Such matters weren't helped by the fact that early on, we worried that our son was slow. For a while, he only spoke one word: mom. Everything was "mom" to him. If he wanted water, he said, "mom." If he was pointing at his father, he said, "mom." When he turned two, he added "shoe" and "water" to his vocabulary. At age three, his language skills still were lacking. My husband worried. "Is he going to be okay?" I told him that I knew our son would catch up. One day, all of a sudden, our son began to speak in complete sentences and from that day he didn't stop.

We also discovered that he had a beautiful voice, like his father. My husband was a very good singer, with a beautiful voice. He was a soloist all the time at our church in America. One of my high school friends visited me to see our son and she said, "Oh, he's so good looking, and he has such a beautiful voice." I always showed off my son's singing in front of my friends! He was shy, but he wanted to please me, so he sang songs.

"Does his father have a good voice, too?" my friend asked.

"Of course!" I said. "You know that my husband is a good singer."

"No, I mean his birth father," my friend said.

"Oh yeah, he was a choir member, too," I said.

Shin Up was a very good-looking boy. When I went out with him alone, people assumed my husband also was good-looking. But if all three of us went out, people looked at us and thought: "Is that your son? He is very good-looking. Where did he get those looks from?" Sometimes I pretended that it was just a quirk, a twist of fate, but most people knew we had adopted. We didn't try to hide it. I didn't fake a pregnancy. We simply explained that we had adopted and that Shin Up was our son.

Our son understood the word "adoption" at an early age but he related it to my work. He knew I worked for an adoption agency and he often saw me on television speaking about it. However, as a child he didn't relate my work to our family or the fact that he was an adopted child. On the other hand, Shinhee learned quickly. Once, not long after the adoption, she came home from school crying and wouldn't tell me what happened. I got a call from her best friend's mother—her best friend also came home crying, but she told her mother what happened. The two girls had gotten into a fight.

"So you brought home a boy from the orphanage?" Shinhee's friend taunted. "You know that's an *orphan*, not your brother, don't you?"

"He is my brother!" Shinhee yelled. "He's my little brother."

"He can't be your brother," the friend said. "He's an orphan!"

They argued and argued. Shinhee thought her friend was calling her a liar and her friend did think Shinhee was a liar. The friend had four siblings, all biological, so she believed that I had to be pregnant and give birth for Shinhee to have a "real" brother. She truly believed that Shinhee was lying. Meanwhile, Shinhee was upset that her friend did not consider Shin Up to be her real brother when Shinhee did.

One day, I was cooking in the kitchen when Shin Up came in from outside and asked, "How does she look?"

I turned around thinking he was talking about someone who had just come by the house. "Is someone at the door?"

"No," he said.

"Then who is 'she'?" I asked.

"The lady who gave me birth," he said.

I was so surprised. Shin Up was only six then. I didn't even use that terminology yet: "the lady who gave me birth." I had no idea where he got that from. All I could say was, "I don't know who she is but I bet she's very pretty because you are very good-looking." Ah, he was so happy with that. That's all he needed to hear then. A few months later, he came back with another question.

"What was her name?" he asked.

"I don't know," I said. "Why?"

"Just curious," he said.

He asked other questions over the next year or two. I wish I had kept track of them all, because at the time it helped me see how a child adjusted to adoption, how he tried to understand it at each stage, and what his perceptions were. It helped me a lot in my job, when I was dealing with adoptive parents.

Shinhee and Shin Up didn't always get along. In fact, about eight months after the adoption, Shinhee ran away from home. Shin Up liked to take his sister's things and ruin them. He tore up her books, broke her pencils and went through all her belongings. When she complained, I told her to lock her door. She did, but her little brother found a way to open it. They were always fighting. I was always upset with my daughter because she was much older, and I lectured her that she shouldn't get into a fight with him when he was so much younger. Actually, what I should have said is "Your brother is misbehaving" instead of blaming her. When she complained to me again, I reminded her of her responsibility as the older sister. "You must be understanding," I said. "He's just a little boy and you are a big girl." One day they had another fight and she was really, really upset. She ran out the door and I called after her.

"Where are you going?" I said.

"I'm not going to stay here any more," she said. "This is a terrible place."

She ran out of the house and down the street. She was running very fast, and this was Seoul, near Itaewon, and very crowded. I was chasing her, but she was very quick. I had to go three or four blocks, because she was really mad and going really fast. I finally caught her and told her that she couldn't run away.

"You are our only daughter," I said.

"No, you can just go adopt another girl if you want," she said. She was furious with me.

After that, I realized how important it was that we pay equal attention to both children. All that time I was worried that Shin Up would feel like the lesser sibling because he was adopted. I didn't realize that I had ended up ignoring my daughter and making her feel secondary. Shin Up's loss I understood; I wasn't as aware of the loss my daughter felt when a new sibling entered the family. I had forgotten that children are jealous and, adopted or not, they need to know that they are loved equally. That's why, after I became a social worker in America working with adoptive parents, I would be sure to tell them how much attention they had to pay to their children who were already in the family at the time of an adoption, whether they had them by birth or by adoption. The existing children always feel they've lost something. They are jealous. The parents' attitude can make all the difference. I think my husband did a better job with it, making sure things were fair between our two kids, and not saying dumb things like "You are older, and he's young, so I'm upset with you, not with him."

Shin Up married first, before Shinhee, so his daughter Alex is now five years old; he has a second child, a son named Aaron, born in 2002, and another one is coming! My daughter Shinhee has a son, Sean, who was born in New York. I am very, very blessed with my children and grandchildren.

Social Work ~
Korea

My first job after college paid about forty dollars per month, and I lost the position before I even went to my first day of work. The American director who initially hired me was impressed with my English speaking ability, as the job required working for an American social work agency. Based on my interview with him I was hired, but a week later, right before I was to start, the director called and told me he could not hire me. When I asked why, he explained that the other social workers knew me from Ewha University (they were older than me) and they felt I was too demanding and strong-headed. They told the director they did not want to work with me.

This was about 1964. I had been married for two years and had an eleven-month-old daughter strapped to my back as I looked for jobs. Remember, we didn't have daycare or babysitters then. Korea still was a very poor post-war country and my husband did not make enough to support all of us, so I was desperate for work. Finally I was hired with International Social Services (ISS). At the time, they had one of the best reputations in Korea. ISS, originally based in Switzerland, was created in the early 1950s, shortly before Holt opened its doors. The agency had an American branch office in New York, and that was the office that sent its delegates to Korea to teach us how to run an adoption agency. When I joined, ISS was considered one of the most professional agencies in Korea. They already were doing child studies, foster care and international adoption for children of racially mixed backgrounds.

Before I joined ISS, they had asked the social work department of Ewha University to help them train their social workers and to recruit new ones who were educated and had social work degrees. My former Human Growth and

Development professor, Mrs. Choi (now Kim), was one of the professors who helped ISS improve its services and develop a more professional reputation. Coincidentally, about a year ago, her own daughter adopted a Korean baby through Children's Home Society with my help. Professor Choi had already completed her work at ISS by the time I got there, but I was happy to know that I again was walking in her footsteps. My co-workers were also college-educated social workers from Ewha University and Yonsei. Yonsei University did not have a social work department, so those graduates came from the English department, as English-speaking skills were necessary for the job.

Back then, ISS was placing only children of racially mixed backgrounds: Korean-Caucasian, Korean-Black, Korean-Filipino, Korean-Thai and so forth. Those were the children in need of homes at the time. With their multiracial background, they did not fit into the rigidly homogeneous Korean culture. The servicemen stationed in Korea during the war who fathered the children had returned to their own homelands, some of them knowing of their progeny and many of them unaware of the children's existence.

The social worker's job was to visit different sites— mostly near the military bases—that were known to have high numbers of mixed-race children living with their birth mothers and ask the mothers if they wanted to place their children for adoption. ISS had three vehicles for the social workers to use and three different drivers, Mr. Kim, Mr. Jeing, and Mr. Lee. Mr. Kim drove the Land Rover, and all of us social workers fought to use this vehicle and the driver because both were considered the best. The terrain was rough and unpaved in the 1960s, so the ride was most comfortable with an all-terrain vehicle. No one wanted to ride with Mr. Lee in the old, used station wagon; the wagon was known for breaking down often, and Mr. Lee for his incessant complaining. The third vehicle was an old Mercury that no one liked or trusted to drive into the countryside or long distances, so we used it mostly for short runs into town when we had to take the children to the hospital for routine check-ups.

Each social worker was assigned a territory and mine was Pyung-taek, near Osan, which was an air force town. Over a period of about twelve to eighteen months, I moved hundreds of those mixed-race children from the town near the military base and into foster care, and eventually placed them for adoption. I had the highest numbers among the ISS social workers at that time, and young and new to the work, I thought this was a good thing. I believed I was helping the children and doing my best at my job. Two-and-a-half years later, after I had moved on to another agency, I went back to the Pyung-taek area to visit and check in on some of the mothers I had met a few years before. There was an obstetrician-gynecology doctor I had worked with who was still there, and I visited her. Because she cared for the ladies in the area, she knew who was pregnant, who had an abortion and who had just delivered. This doctor believed that adoption was a good thing for mixed-race children and so she helped me by giving me names of mothers who had recently delivered. When I visited her two years later, she confessed that in the past, whenever I came into town, all the mothers in the area panicked. They yelled: "Quick! Hide your children! Mrs. Shim is coming!" All that time, I did not know that the mothers were afraid of me, afraid that I was going to make them agree that their children should be placed for adoption.

Although I was a college-educated social worker, the agencies back then were pioneers in the field of adoption and foster care and did not have standards developed yet, so social workers like me did not have enough proper training, education and standards. I misunderstood my job and thought I was supposed to make the birth mothers relinquish their children; I pushed those mothers to sign the papers. Of course, I did not walk into town and just grab the children. The way I tried was to convince those mothers that their children were better off coming with me and being adopted internationally. I told them: "What is your plan for the baby? What do you think the baby's future will be in Korea? Koreans will not accept your child. How can your child live?" I reminded those mothers of Korean ways, and how mixed-race children are not welcome in Korean society; they would be ridiculed, teased, and rejected by their own people. The mothers always said: "But he told me he loved me. I think he will marry me." The birth mothers always wanted to believe the men, even though they never provided a few dollars here and there to support the baby, or even so much as sent a post card. Korean people almost never say "I love you" but the birth mothers wanted to believe that's what the soldiers said. "I love you, I want to marry you, I want to raise our baby." Waiting for these words is why many birth mothers raised their children on their own as long as they could. But when a child was older than seven, most of the time the adoption agency couldn't find adoptive parents. I tried to explain that to the women. Believe me, I wasn't trying to separate mother and child; I really believed, in my youth and naïveté, that I was doing the best I could do for these children. I was giving them a better chance. That was how social work agencies were in Korea back then. We were young women, fresh out of college, trying to do the best we could at our jobs with little instruction and training. Back then, the area of social work was relatively new to Korea and so we had no models to follow.

Another program of ISS was foster care. In fact, my agency was the first to start such a program. Think about it. This was Korea in the sixties. Who in the world in Korea would welcome a Korean-Caucasian baby into their home? No married couples would take them because they wanted to have birth children to continue the family name. Older married couples didn't want to take them, because people might think their own daughter was the mother of this child, and they had to take care of the baby. Single men and women did not want to care for these children, even temporarily, because their neighbors and friends might mistake the child as their own and ruin their chances for future marriage and raising a family of their own. So early on, no one participated in our program—except some families who lived near the American military bases. People believed the children were theirs. I was living in Itaewon at the time, but not in the central part where all the entertainment venues were. Rather, I was living in a quieter back neighborhood that was lower middle class. All of the residents in my neighborhood were elderly Koreans. When I saw all the children placed in foster care in the area of the "entertainers," I knew I had to do something. That atmosphere was not a healthy one in which to raise a small child, so I started a movement in my own neighborhood. I asked if any of the elderly Koreans would be willing to take in a small mixed-race child. They did, and they loved those children dearly. The elderly foster parents didn't disgrace themselves by taking in these children because of their age;

others knew the children couldn't possibly be the offspring of an elderly couple or man or woman, and these people were past the age of caring what others thought. They had nothing to lose and lots of love to gain.

I continued to place children in foster homes in Itaewon but never told people that I was an adoption social worker. If the ladies in the area knew I was a social worker, I would suddenly have had abandoned babies on my doorstep by the dozens. As it was, I came across plenty of abandoned children in that area, and I followed the protocol at the time: report the abandoned child to the police station, then take it to the agency reception center and later place the child for adoption.

During the early years of my career, Korea remained a very poor country. My own home did not have running water; we carried buckets to the public city pump for water. Back and forth, back and forth. Even if we had the money to pay for plumbing, it wasn't available where we lived. I had my baby daughter during this time. We did not have disposable diapers, and our cloth diapers were of a rough material. The cloth did not dry easily; it was big and long and extra thick. I felt like I was always washing diapers, and if it rained, our house was filled with wet dripping cloth that took forever to dry. Also, milk was not available. My husband and I made enough money to buy a few goods, but there were no goods to buy—no milk, no sugar, nothing. There was powdered milk but it wasn't of good quality and often was smuggled, so the price was higher than it was worth. If we did get some powdered milk, it was the American kind, which was terrible. Korean powdered milk is sweet; eventually we learned to add sugar to the American kind. I always worried about where to buy our next supply of milk for the baby, rice, and other foods. Most of the time, we subsisted on rice gruel.

I breast fed my daughter for more than a year, which was typical, and in a malnourished country, that was her best source of nutrition. During the time I was breast-feeding my daughter, I was working as a social worker, visiting Pyung-taek, Pusan, and Taegu. Some of these places were in the poorest of areas. I remember houses made of mud and clay with cheap straw roofs. These were in the countryside. The "entertainers" lived in these small, one-room huts. Inside, the huts were small and dark and contained a single bed. Cramped in the small room with the mother and her baby, I tried to talk to these mothers about relinquishing their children. Many of these mothers didn't make enough money to buy powdered milk, and they were unable to breast feed so often I offered their children my breasts.

Back at the agency, we had many infants in our care before we found them foster homes or families willing to adopt. Most social workers back then were unmarried young women. When the babies cried and rejected their bottles, these young ladies handed the infants to me. I was a new mother with milk-filled breasts. Soon, I became known as the breast-feeding lady. In fact, my breasts became so engorged with milk that I had trouble moving my arms. My daughter wouldn't take more milk; she got diarrhea from too much so I had to get rid of the excess. One day I remember standing in my backyard, ridding my breasts of all the extra milk when the neighbor boy saw me. He ran home and told his mom, and she ran out, yelling, "Don't throw it away!" Her son was malnourished because she couldn't breast-feed, so I gave him my excess milk. I didn't mind. At the time, I didn't have enough extra money or food to give to those in need, but I could offer them my milk. This was a relief to me as well; I didn't have to walk around in pain from too much milk.

Not everyone approved of my breast-feeding, especially when I breast-fed a mixed-race child in public. One time I had to visit several areas in the countryside for work. I was on my way back from Taegu and decided to take the train. However, I was carrying luggage and six or seven babies that had been relinquished. I held one in each arm, had another on my back but no more room for the others. Plus, I still needed an arm to hold my umbrella, for it was raining, and I had luggage to carry. Impossible. I had a friend who lived in Taegu. He was a young man who had graduated two years before me from Seoul University and worked for a textile company. On previous trips when I needed help, I gave him a call. "Mr. Kim? This is Hyun Sook. I'm in Taegu and need some help. Could you please come and meet me at the train station?" As always, he came to help me out.

Later, he joked that I was ruining him. "Because of you, Mrs. Shim, my friend, I can never marry! People see me with you and all these mixed-race children and think they are mine!" He laughed, but I didn't. I hadn't stopped to think what that meant. To me, I was simply doing my job. I knew people looked down on us on the train; old ladies tsked-tsked me as I breast-fed the babies on the ride back into Seoul. Still, I paid the stares and disapproving looks little attention; the babies were always crying and always hungry and wanting their mothers, so most of my attention was on them. One after another, I fed those babies, because even though they were of different races they were all very hungry. Later, I apologized to my friend; his predicament was more serious because he still was single. I never called him again to help. He married later, I heard; maybe because I stopped calling him and putting him in such an embarrassing situation. On the other hand, my husband strongly believed that I did the right thing by feeding those babies at my breasts.

Itaewon in the sixties was not as developed as it is today. Some shops had begun to spring up for the American soldiers, but they were small and few. The same was true of the pubs and nightclubs; only a few existed back then. However, the Red Light District did exist then. Most "entertainers" either worked at establishments in the Red Light District or solicited business in front of the army bases. They were not allowed to solicit in the public residential streets, only the ones in front of the military bases.

The clothing shops sold clothes from factories that had rejected the goods for regular retail sale, and that's how people got a good bargain. When I lived there with my husband and daughter, I never shopped there; most Koreans didn't until the shops expanded and began to sell brand-name items at a discount, and fake Rolex watches and Gucci bags. Although Americans shopped there back then, few shopkeepers spoke English. Not until about 1975 did Itaewon become more international; now all the merchants speak English. I still go there now to buy interesting items and gifts for my American friends.

In the sixties, Itaewon bars and clubs had American names like they do today: Paradise Club, Lucky Seven Club. These were considered ritzier names than the establishments located in the countryside areas, like Pyung-taek; clubs out there were given American names, like Texas Club.

The women who worked the clubs sometimes arranged

"contracts" with American soldiers. Girls who had contracts were considered fortunate. This meant that they could count on a steady income from a single soldier and didn't have to hustle every night, soliciting new business. These women also were able to live in certain residential neighborhoods but had to pay higher rent to the landlords. Otherwise, most "entertainers" had to live in housing areas designated for such women. Up until about the late sixties, women in their thirties could make a living as entertainers but as post-war poverty continued, more and more young girls entered the industry. Often, these were girls from poor families who worked in factories, fifteen or sixteen hours a day, for little pay. Unable to support their families on such meager wages, these girls became "entertainers," and that eventually pushed the veterans over the age of thirty-five out of business. Many of the "entertainers" got pregnant and decided to place their babies for adoption. The highest number of babies with mixed racial backgrounds was 1964 to 1969, then the number started getting smaller. By 1971, Korean adoption agencies had a much greater number of full-blooded Korean babies for overseas adoption.

My early years as a social worker left a particular impression on me, maybe because the work was new to me, maybe because I was so young and still a bit naïve, and maybe because I had chosen a career that would break my heart over and over.

There are so many people behind the scenes of adoption, and I do not mean the paid staff of adoption agencies; I am talking about the birth mothers and the children. These are the people I really work for; the ones who have pushed me to work harder and harder and become better and better—not just as a social worker but as a human being—with each passing year. And because of them I have become an even better storyteller, for they have passed on to me the job of giving voice to their stories.

(Please note that in some instances, names have been changed to safeguard the privacy of the individuals and their families.)

Bad teeth

Bobby's birth mother was a very polite woman who had two Korean children before the war. Her husband and mother were killed during the war so she was left with the responsibility of supporting her own family and her husband's family after the war. She had been a housewife with no formal training or education, so she became an "entertainer" at age 34. Many young girls had to do this. Most had no choice; it was the only way to survive, especially for the girls who were runaways or had to support their families and children.

Now, let me explain something before I continue. On agency reports we referred to these women as "entertainers" because we began to receive complaints from adoptive parents. Early on, we wrote "prostitute" on the adoption papers in reference to the mother's background. About a year into my career, we began to hear complaints. The adoptive parents began to ask for the translation of that scribbled Korean word. When we explained that it meant "prostitute" or "lover," they became upset. From then on, we began to refer to the mother's occupation as "entertainer."

The best situation for these "entertainers" was to get a "contract" with an American soldier. The soldiers were given extra money each month for miscellaneous expenses, and many used it for their entertainment. The Korean girls knew this and tried to set up an arrangement in which they became one soldier's "girl." This meant that she didn't have to work the streets or clubs at night; she worked for that one soldier. He could depend on a regular girl and she could depend on a steady income. This also relieved the fear of contracting sexually transmitted diseases and the girl's fear of being mugged, beaten or raped while working the streets at night. Contracts were safe, in a sense. Of course, a contract did not mean that the young girl escaped the emotional scars of her profession. In some instances, this situation had longer-term effects. If a soldier was stationed for more than a year, the result often was a baby, and then false promises of marriage on the soldier's part. In the end, the girl often was left behind with another mouth to feed and no hope for marriage.

Bobby's mother was one of those entertainers who didn't drink or smoke. Her son was part Caucasian, and she did not want to place him for adoption. She loved him and could not bear to send him away when he was an infant, but when I met her, Bobby was nearing school age and his mother knew she could not send him to a Korean school. He would've been discriminated against because he was not one-hundred percent Korean. His mother told me she cried every night over her son's fate. When I came to her, she knew she had no choice left. "I have met you now. You seem like an honest person. I know that you will do a good job for my son," she said to me. Whenever I think of her, I get tears in my eyes.

Because Bobby was already four years old, I had trouble finding a good placement for him. Most adoptive parents wanted infants. I wrote to the New York office of ISS and asked them to help me find a family for Bobby. They found a family, and so I went back to Bobby's mother to have her sign the relinquishment papers. She cried, out of sadness and joy, but she signed the papers. Usually, Koreans use a specially made wooden stamp for signatures, called a chop, or at least a pen, but she had nothing like that to use, so she signed the papers with her thumbprint, using her lipstick as the ink.

"I have signed this paper," she said. "I will never reclaim this child and I know I now have no rights. He is not my child anymore, and I will never ask about him."

That was the agreement back then. The birth parent(s) had to completely relinquish the child to us; officially, legally, they were no longer the child's parents. We did it that way back then to make sure the parents understood what they were doing, and that the papers made it final. The agencies would keep their identities secret, and they, like their child, would be given another chance to start again. And now, here we are, the same social workers back in Korea, knocking on these parents' doors, showing our faces on television and asking them to come forward because their child is looking for them. Some birth mothers feel that we, the agencies and social workers, have broken the agreement we had with them, but we felt it was necessary to do this for the sake of the adopted persons.

Bobby was brought to Seoul and placed in foster care until his adoption was final. We completed his child study information, his background and that of his mother, as well as his overall physical, mental and emotional development. He had bad teeth, so I included that in the report. Because of that, I think someone requested that we do more tests to make sure Bobby had no developmental difficulties. I insisted that he was a very bright boy who understood everything; his bad teeth could be fixed and had nothing to do with his mental abilities. To prove this, I asked Bobby if he knew why he was going to America. He said he was being adopted. I asked him if he knew what adoption was. He replied that his new parents were not the ones who were pregnant with him but they would be the ones who would raise him and therefore become his "real" parents. I asked him where his Korean mother fit into the picture. He told me that she could not raise him because he looked different, and that's why he had to go live in America. After my report back, no one questioned this boy's mental abilities. They agreed; he was a very smart four-year-old.

I was twenty-six when I placed Bobby, and today, I still miss him. Back then I never wondered what would happen to some of those children. I was just doing my job. But now, sometimes I catch myself thinking about them, the ones like Bobby. He would be so much older now. Can you imagine?

Broken promises

Annie's mother lived in Itaewon and was a chubby girl, but cute. Her daughter was one-and-a-half years old, Korean and Caucasian, with dark brown eyes and a long pretty face. I promised Annie's mother that I would find a good family for her daughter, but I did not explain the details of the entire adoption process to her, or that a Korean social worker doesn't have much influence over social workers at the New York agency. It was the U.S. agency that made the decision about the family with whom a baby would be placed. The fact was that my promise was mostly to console her, to ease her fears, and not one I could necessarily keep. In America, a social worker could promise to find the best possible family for a child and might be better able to keep that promise.

Unlike most cases, where we took the child from the mother as soon as the papers were signed, the agency agreed to let Annie's mother care for her up until she was adopted. This was a mistake we later regretted. At the time, we reasoned that Annie's mother took excellent care of her little girl and she was still able to breast-feed. She also insisted that we not place her daughter in foster care. This woman promised me that she would not argue or put up a fight when we came for Annie as long as we found adoptive parents who were college educated. To Koreans, "college educated" meant that they would be the best, and wonderful. She was upset that we wanted to place her daughter with a family where the mother had a high school diploma, not a college degree. I asked the American agency to find a different family for Annie.

The American agency was very upset with me. It was 1964 and there were not as many female college graduates as we wanted. In addition, Annie had some problems and finding her a family would be difficult enough without the additional promises I had made to the mother, that Annie would go to a college-educated couple. Still, I did my best. I felt I had to respect the birth mother's wishes; my part was easier than hers. She was giving her child to strangers. At least I could ensure that they were the kind of people she would want to raise her daughter. The birth mother felt that she herself would not be in this situation if she had a better education, and that's why she wanted Annie to have a mother who was very well educated.

The American agency sent a long letter that described how wonderful this particular adoptive mother was, and included her letters of reference. They also told how the adoptive parents planned an excellent education for Annie.

That new information greatly comforted the birth mother, and Annie went to that family after all.

Annie's case was a hard lesson for me. For a long time I felt guilty about what I was doing, making promises I couldn't always keep and trying to get the "best" according to the birth mother's expectations, even when that was almost impossible, or at least not within my power.

White-haired hunger

The OB/GYN doctor I worked with told me about a mother who had recently delivered a partly black baby boy, and that she might relinquish him for adoption. When I went to the woman's house, I saw that she was very ill, and both she and her baby were starving. This mother was an "entertainer" who had slept with a black soldier—once; after that, she could never be with a Caucasian soldier anymore. This was in the sixties and prejudice against blacks was common, not just among Koreans but also among Caucasians. So once it was known that she had been with a black soldier, the woman could not get a long-term contract with a soldier. No Caucasian men would touch her, and according to her, the black soldiers didn't stay in Korea as long as the white ones to make a long-term contract. They didn't want steady "girlfriends"; they only wanted one night. So her life was very difficult.

The mother was forced to work the streets. Her income was sparse and unpredictable, and in time she became sick from malnutrition and then was unable to work. I asked the mother what she fed the baby, if she was able to breast-feed. She said she could not because the men would not come to her; they didn't like the leaking milk. An older lady took care of her child and fed the baby rice gruel; she was too old to breast-feed herself and the mother was too poor to buy milk. The baby was starving to death. And strangely, the boy had completely white hair.

I placed the baby in foster care, believing he probably would die. We got the baby medical care, and I asked the doctor how this baby—a Korean-black baby—had white hair. He explained to me that it was due to malnutrition. Once the baby had been in foster care for a while and properly nourished, his hair turned black. Eventually, he was adopted by an air force sergeant stationed in Okinawa, Japan; he was black. We were fortunate; back then we did not recruit enough African-American couples to adopt these babies.

Mixed up

We used to use abbreviations for adoption files that indicated a child's race. The most common ones went like this:

K-C: Korean-Caucasian

K-B or K-N: Korean-black or Korean-Negro (this was in the sixties)

K-P: Korean Filipino

K-T: Korean Turkish (they also helped fight the war)

I was in charge of placing a very pretty baby with curly, almost-blonde hair, fair skin and light brown eyes. She was an abandoned baby, left at an orphanage. At that time, the orphanages contacted us with abandoned children and asked us to place them for adoption. We received little background information on these children and no racial background information, so we played a sort of guessing game in these cases.

When I placed the blonde baby girl, I designated her race as K-C, and she was adopted by a white American couple. The next week, I received an angry letter from our New York office asking me to explain myself. According to the letter, the adoptive parents were furious with me and the agency for giving them a black baby.

"Why did you do such a thing?" the director asked.

"I didn't know," I said. "Look at the picture."

The baby, indeed, had curly almost-blonde hair, fair skin and light brown eyes.

"I thought this baby was white," I said. "How could I know?"

Here I was, in my twenties, expected to guess the race of mixed-race babies. I had never been to America at that point in my life; all of my life I had grown up around just Koreans. The only time I saw people of another race was during the war, but I had no idea who was mixed. I didn't understand that some blacks—like this baby girl—could look like a white person. Besides, who can tell the exact race of a baby that is mixed? No one gave us any ideas or suggestions. I was expected to guess, I told the director. Maybe if I lived in America for many years and saw many people of all different races and mixes, I might learn how to tell, but I live in Korea, I said. How could I know?

The office in New York wrote back and said they were no longer upset; they understood the confusion. However, they had to place the baby with a different family because white couples did not want to adopt black children, even mixed, back then in America. That changed, of course, later—much later.

Happy and sad

One other case I had as a young social worker in Korea involved an older mother, close to forty years old, who also was an "entertainer". She had two daughters: ages six and three. The older girl had freckles all over, which by Korean standards is not so attractive; the younger girl had a freckle-free face and was cuter and prettier than her older sister.

The mother, a thin, unattractive woman, wanted me to find the girls a home together. If I could not find a family that would take both of them, as sisters, she would not relinquish them, she told me. I frowned. Adoptions were still so new, and no one wanted to adopt more than one. I knew how hard it was going to be to find such a couple, so we agreed to let the mother continue to care for her daughters until we had secured a new family for both of them.

We were lucky enough to find a couple who was willing to take two sisters. The adoptive parents were close to forty years old, and at that time we didn't place children with anyone over age forty; they also were college professors. The birth mother was very pleased. She relinquished the girls, happily and sadly. Happy that they would have a better life in America with two educated parents, and sad that they had no chance for a good life—marriage, especially, as mixed-race girls—in Korea, at her side.

I used to visit this mother every so often, years after the adoption. She never regretted her decision; she only regretted her situation. "I will have sorrow until my death," she told me. Although she knew her daughters were better off in America, she could not help but feel pain for the loss of her daughters, wishing and wondering what their lives might have been like had they lived in a country that accepted them as they were, together.

Sad as cases like these were, the saddest cases were of those who could not be adopted. I had many mothers ask me to try and find homes in America for their children, but these children were too old. Americans only adopted girls up to age five and boys up to age three, and only children who were K-C. No other mixes. Most five- and-six-year-olds had a hard time being placed for adoption. Sometimes, I would see older children in the orphanages and they would beg me to send them to America. "Adopt me! Adopt me!" they cried. These were children who were old enough to go to school and knew of the discrimination they faced the longer they stayed in Korea. "Half-breed! Half-breed!" the other children yelled. The older mixed-race children were isolated from mainstream Korean society, and so they lashed out. They hit and kicked and beat up others; this was how they survived. Their mothers didn't know what to do, knowing that their children could not grow up always fighting. These were the same mothers who refused to relinquish their infants for adoption, and as the children grew and met up with rigid Korean society, the mothers fully understood their mistake: they should have allowed their babies to be adopted.

After 1967, there were fewer mixed-race children available for adoption. Either the babies had already been placed or they were now too old for adoption. ISS, which did only mixed-race adoptions, closed its doors in 1966. Holt, Korean Social Services and Social Welfare Society all continued their international adoption programs. By 1970, overseas demand for full-blooded Korean infants grew—but not before in-country adoptions began.

In 1967 I was working for the Christian Adoption Program of Korea (CAPOK), which was a missionary extension of the Christian Reformed Church of Michigan.

That year, CAPOK placed as many as one hundred-plus children. In Korea. I was surprised; I didn't think native Koreans would adopt. CAPOK was one of the first agencies to begin an in-country adoption program; the others followed with similar programs in the early seventies.

In its early days, CAPOK operated mainly as a missionary agency. Although they started to do adoptions in 1962, these were unofficial. Some people just came to them and asked if they were caring for a child who was available for adoption. There was not much paperwork yet, no legal process. There were simple home studies, simple medical check-ups and very few questions asked. Many times, the babies were just given to those who asked.

When I joined CAPOK as an assistant supervisor, they had become far more organized, even more organized than ISS. With CAPOK, I learned proper social work fundamentals and procedures—and saw that all along I had been doing my job very wrong. At ISS I used to push those mothers to relinquish their children for adoption. Working for CAPOK, I learned that a social worker never pushes a mother into giving up her child. I learned that the mother should only sign the paperwork because she wants to and needs to, not because I tell her that it is the right thing to do for her child. After I learned this, I went back to some of those areas I used to visit frequently, like Pyung-taek, and visited the birth mothers I had visited years before. I asked them: "Do you blame me? Are you angry with me for pushing you too much to relinquish your babies?" One mother told me: "Are you kidding? If you didn't push we wouldn't have sent them overseas, and later we would regret that decision. You had to push us; we could not make such a difficult decision ourselves."

CAPOK's adoption program was just one service it provided. Originally, their missionaries were sent to the countryside to help the poor farmers and provide health care in rural areas. Once there, the missionaries discovered the growing need for families to adopt all the abandoned children, and so they began adoption services. Eventually, they needed Korean social workers who spoke both English and Korean to help interpret and supervise.

The director was Ms. Spoelstra, an adoption social worker who was sent to Korea (from Colorado) by the Christian Reformed Mission in Michigan. She needed an assistant. I was the only person they found who fit all the necessary credentials: I spoke English and Korean, possessed a social work degree and had worked with another professional adoption agency. As Ms. Spoelstra's assistant supervisor, I did a lot of translating for her and helped her supervise the other social workers, some of whom I knew from Ewha University. Meanwhile, I learned the Western way of doing adoptions and picked up a new set of professional skills. At the time, Ms. Spoelstra was the only social worker in Korea who specialized in child welfare. We were also the only agency that did in-country adoptions.

Ms. Spoelstra was active in a group called Korean American Voluntary Agencies (KAVA). Many different organizations with delegates in Korea were involved: Foster Parents Plan, Christian Children's Plan, Save the Children's Fund, and so on. As a group, these agencies had a stronger voice and more influence in Korea, so they hosted conferences and exchanged ideas and information. Ms. Spoelstra always took me with her to these meetings. Outside of the office, I learned more about this tall Dutch lady who was my boss. She was not married but was very mature and probably was one of the best Christian models I have ever met. She was so generous to all of us at the agency. When we had placed two hundred infants in Korean homes, she invited us to an expensive ham dinner—and American chocolate for dessert, a rare treat for young Korean women at the time. Sometimes she took me to the train station and treated me to a real American hamburger at the army personnel services restaurant. Oh, that was so good! Other times she would invite us to her home for holiday parties, another big treat for us. My Korean co-workers and I would dress in our *hanboks* and wear make-up for the special event. When one of the male Canadian supervisors saw us, he said we looked like completely different people with make-up on; he barely recognized us. At work, we never wore make-up; it just wasn't practical in our line of work. We had to wake up so early in the morning and run around all day; make-up wasn't important, day to day.

When I first started at CAPOK, they were renting a few office rooms in the Old Severance Hospital near the Seoul train station. The building was old and dark and made of brick. Few people knew the hospital was there, and other companies rented office space in that building as well, so CAPOK was not very visible. In those days, the social workers often sat idly with no work to do. There were no phones to make calls, and no one came in to inquire about adopting a baby. Finally, after about a month of waiting, they began to receive a few applications for baby boys.

Those were also the days when agencies had no hard-and-fast rules to guide them through the tangled web that was in-country adoptions. Every case presented a new and challenging problem. Often, Korean wives came to us alone, without their husbands, and asked for a newborn baby. They did not want their husbands to know of the adoption; these women tried to pass off these babies as their own. Back then, husbands did not go to the hospital delivery room with the expectant mothers, so the fathers never witnessed their child's birth. This was one way women could trick their husbands. Another way was to fake pregnancy. The wife would tell her husband she was pregnant and they must sleep in separate rooms because if they slept together, she might miscarry. This was especially effective if there had already been a miscarriage. The husbands didn't know any better, so they agreed; they never saw or touched their wives' stomachs. Also, most Korean houses did not have indoor plumbing during this time so people went to the public bath houses to bathe, and this meant that a husband never saw his wife's bare stomach—and never knew that the bulge underneath her clothing was simply extra padding. For wives who could not become pregnant—or had not given birth to a son—this was a necessary deception. Remember, bloodlines were very important to Koreans, so the wives had to make their husbands believe that the newborn baby was their birth child.

Early on, we allowed this practice to take place but later we changed it. We required that adopting parents must come together and both must agree to the adoption. Part of our reason for this demand was to gather some proof that the adopting couple was legally married. Back then, there was no Korean law that required adopting couples to prove that they were married. Those who lived in the countryside often had no such proof. They didn't think it mattered to register their marriage legally, because there was no practical reason to do so until they had a baby to register. (Actually, my husband

and I did the same thing with our legal paperwork: our wedding date and my daughter's birth date were registered on the same day.)

In that way, our agency's rule helped legal marriage, and by 1970, the government officially announced that adopting parents must be legally married and show a marriage license as proof in order to adopt. You see, a common problem was that the men who lived in the countryside would frequently visit the city and legally marry a young city girl, despite having a "wife" in the countryside. We did not want couples like this adopting. Following the legalization of marriages, we began requiring medical records from both adoptive parents. There were many cases of tuberculosis (TB) back then so couples brought in x-rays to show that they did not have the disease. Unfortunately, x-rays were all we had to go on for proof of health, and the clinics that provided this service only did x-rays and blood tests of the men. For many years, we already had complete physicals for foster mothers, and many years later we checked on the whole adoptive family, but at that time we only asked adoptive parents for some basic information.

So in those early days of in-country adoptions, we encountered all kinds of strange situations and we had to make decisions based on individual cases. For instance, once we had a college-educated woman and her husband come to our agency and ask to adopt a baby girl. Then, most couples wanted to adopt a baby boy. Because they had made such an unusual request—and we were happy to see a couple want a baby girl—we picked the prettiest baby for them to adopt. She had big, big eyes. A few hours later the wife returned. She had a terror-struck look on her face and asked if she could exchange the baby for one with smaller more slanted eyes. She explained that as soon as her mother-in-law saw the baby with big eyes, the older woman exclaimed, "Yah! How in the world can this baby have such big eyes when you both have such small eyes? Koreans are not supposed to have such big eyes. You must return this baby or people will think this is a Korean-Caucasian baby, and that would be impossible!" That was the only time we exchanged a baby. You see, we messed up in giving them a child that did not share their physical traits. Koreans adopting back then wanted a child they could pass as their birth child because society would not have been equally accepting of an adopted child.

Another time a woman came to us and said she needed a baby right away. She had announced her delivery date as the following week and now she needed to deliver. We hurried to find an infant but there weren't many newborns, and she wanted a boy, which made our search more difficult. Everyone wanted a baby boy. Luckily, someone had called us earlier and asked us to come by and pick up an abandoned child. The infant was a boy and we told the woman that we needed to do a medical exam first. She was in a hurry and said not to worry; she would take full responsibility if the baby was not healthy. We gave her the baby and two days later she was back in our office with the child. During those two days, she had taken the baby to her doctor and found out that he was not expected to live much longer. All of his internal organs were in all the wrong places. I think the baby did die and the woman had to tell everyone that her son had died of internal complications. She and her husband had to wait another year to adopt because she had to fake her pregnancy all over again. If only she had waited just one more day so we could have done a full medical exam, she would have been saved all that heartache. After that, we learned our lesson and never placed a baby without a complete medical exam, no matter what the situation.

Have you ever heard of "doggy-hole" adoptions? That may not be the best translation into English, but this was a common practice in those early days of in-country adoptions. You see, the old-time traditional belief was that if you wanted a baby, you announced whether you wanted a baby girl or boy out loud so the neighbors could hear you, and once you made the announcement, poof! There was a baby at your door within a short time. In reality, someone left the couple a baby she might otherwise have abandoned. Of course, the person did not walk up to a stranger's door and place the baby on the doorstep. Back then, people had fences around their houses, and in the fence, there was usually a hole big enough for a dog to crawl through. Hence the name "doggy-hole." People abandoned their babies that way, by placing the infant through the hole in the fence and into the yard of a stranger, where the baby would be safe until the resident discovered him.

When a baby was abandoned this way and the couple decided to keep the child, this was considered a "doggy-hole" adoption and the child was recognized as that family's "real" child. That meant that the parents could give that child their family name, and the child could inherit his parents' material wealth after they died. Remember that this was a time when adopted children were not considered a couple's real children by certain laws, and so adopted children could not inherit an adoptive parent's estate. The logic behind this law was to protect the rights of the birth parents. If the birth parents ever came back and claimed an adopted child, the law back then favored the birth parents instead of the adoptive parents, so for many couples who adopted in those early days, there was always the fear that the birth parents might come back and reclaim the child. Nowadays the laws protect the adoptive parents and let them pass on their family name to their adopted child, but that wasn't the case in those days. In fact, around 1972 or 1973, I had to go to court to argue a case in which the birth mother wanted to reclaim her child, who had been adopted. I tried to explain to the court that in-country adoptions were just as important to develop as international adoptions, but the agencies could not do this if the courts allowed birth parents to reclaim their birth children at any time, even when the child had been legally adopted. We lost that case; back then the court favored the birth parent. After that, we sent lawyers instead of social workers to argue cases.

After the war, doggy-hole adoptions were considered an old tradition, and adoption agencies became the path to adoption. So many people were abandoning babies and children at any door that no one knew if someone had asked for such a child. However, there was one mother-in-law who believed that doggy-hole adoptions were the best way to have a family; she distrusted adoption agencies and orphanages. Her son and his wife came to us, behind the mother-in-law's back, and explained the situation. They did not believe in doggy-hole adoptions but their mother did not want them to adopt from an agency, so they asked us to help them. That way, both sides could be happy. They gave us a specific date to let a child be abandoned on their doorstep, based on what the fortune teller told them. (Koreans consult fortune tellers to find out the best date for important events such as marriage, moving and so on.)

The social worker handling the case asked me if this was something we could do. I asked our American supervisor and she said absolutely not; that was abandonment. We could not participate in such a thing, she said. I explained to the supervisor that it would be okay in this case because it was important to understand the Korean custom and respect it. In the end, that child would be adopted into a family that would love him, I said. Finally, our supervisor agreed, and the social worker in charge of the case dressed in plain, old clothing on the designated night. She wrapped the baby in a blanket and pinned his birth date and time of birth to the blanket, then went out to the couple's house. Rather than take the agency car, she took a taxi to make sure that the mother would not see her and become suspicious. When she arrived at the house, she snuck up to the house and put the baby at the door, and then ran and hid. She tried to listen for some sign that someone had discovered the baby but heard nothing. No one stirred. The social worker knew that this was the night the couple told her to come and didn't understand why they did not come out to the door. Meanwhile, the couple was talking to the mother and knew that the baby was being dropped off at that time. The problem was that they could not get up and go outside for no reason; they had no excuse for checking the yard. Finally, the social worker understood what the problem was and came out from her hiding place. She went back to the house, opened the blanket, and pinched the baby to make him cry. Then she ran away again to hide. This time, she heard a loud voice: "There's a baby crying outside the house!" It was the mother-in-law; she believed the tradition had come true.

The family was very happy, and when their baby son's first birthday came, the wife had a celebration and invited the social worker who had helped them adopt the baby. Of course, the social worker could not reveal her true identity, so she and the wife, both of the same age, pretended to be old school friends. The baby's grandmother never knew what her son and daughter-in-law had done; she happily believed that her family was blessed with good luck.

Another strange request happened in the early seventies. A mother-in-law and her son came running into our agency asking for a newborn baby boy—that day. They explained that the man's wife had fainted in the delivery room when she learned that she had given birth to her third daughter; she wanted so badly to have a boy that she told her husband she wanted to die. They wanted to adopt a newborn baby boy that afternoon and return to the hospital before the wife gained consciousness. We asked them how they would explain such a thing to the wife, and they told us that they would tell the wife she had given birth to twins but had fainted before anyone could tell her that the other child was a boy. Luckily, we had a healthy newborn baby boy and the mother-in-law and her son rushed back to the hospital with our social worker. The wife was lying on her hospital bed with eyes closed but she was conscious; she just didn't want to open her eyes and deal with her disappointment. So the mother-in-law shouted: "Open your eyes! Don't be disappointed! See? You gave birth to a baby boy. You had twins!" The wife opened her eyes. "What?" she said, in disbelief. "Here is your baby boy," the husband said and presented his wife with their son. The woman was so happy.

We kept that family's secret but insisted that the social worker who helped them check up on the child on his first birthday. The father agreed and invited her to their home. During the visit, the social worker saw that the mother gave the little girl (the "twin") powdered milk but fed her "twin" brother breast milk. The mother ignored the girl and showered attention and praise on the boy—even though he was the one who was adopted, which, of course, the mother didn't know. Back at the agency, the social worker reported what she saw to our director, and the director told her to go back and tell the mother-in-law that the mother must give both of her "twin" children equal treatment or the secret would be revealed. From then on, the grandmother made sure the mother followed our advice.

When Korean women still wore the traditional Korean dresses, *hanboks*, they could easily hide unwanted pregnancies. The dresses already ballooned out, so no one saw a woman's stomach growing underneath. Often, rich families would build a small house behind the main one and have their pregnant, unwed daughter live there—in hiding—until the baby was born. So who were these unwed mothers? Sometimes they were women who had lovers and became pregnant. Others might have been raped. Some might have been servants, and they didn't want their child to inherit their social status. There wasn't any documentation on them back then; society demanded that they hide their shame. This was when babies were often abandoned for the "doggy-hole" adoptions.

Unwed mothers have been part of Korea's history, going back several thousand years. One of the most famous kings of the ancient Shilla Dynasty impregnated his girlfriend before they became husband and wife. The law of that time mandated that the woman be killed—burned alive—if she did not reveal who was the father of her unborn baby. This great Shilla king watched in horror and fear as his girlfriend was tied to the stake, and before they burned her alive, he shouted out, "She is carrying my child." She then became the king's wife.

In 1969, before CAPOK started the first unwed mothers program, I did some research with a college student on the reclamation of abandoned babies at Seoul City Reception Center/Children's Hospital, where all abandoned babies found in Seoul were taken. Of about 87 babies, approximately 80 percent were reclaimed by their unwed birth mothers because the birth fathers pressured them to get the babies back. Some of the men wanted to continue the relationship and include the baby, and some were married men who wanted to take their birth sons back to their wives, and register the son legally. The unwed mothers would often prefer this for their babies, because at least it would be a better life for their children. Sometimes a man would have a legal wife in the city, and a mistress in the country. The country woman would have to abandon her baby, because she could not afford to take care of it by herself. The birth father would come back, demand that the baby be reclaimed, but then leave again, so the mother would have to abandon the baby a second time. Often the babies did not fare well in these circumstances, and some of them died. It was a great regret for us.

Based on these findings, CAPOK started its program for unwed mothers so that we could help them help themselves, and reduce the number of abandonments, as the death rate for the babies was terribly high. In the first six months of the program, we successfully placed sixty-seven healthy children for adoption while helping the unwed birth mothers with counseling to work out their feelings of guilt, and to start a new life for themselves after making an adoption plan for their babies. Later, we started to collect all kinds of social background and health information about the birth mother and the baby while they were in our program. By 1970, I had begun to compile statistics on all of our unwed mothers. The youngest unwed mother at the time was twelve years old; a few more were fourteen. We also had quite a few in junior high, but most unwed mothers were poor, uneducated girls, mostly under the age of 20, who worked in factories or came from the countryside.

In one case, a fifth-grade girl rolled over one night, sick with stomach pains. Her parents took her to a large hospital and she delivered a baby. Her parents were really shocked, as was the young girl. She had no idea she was even pregnant; her parents never knew either. Young as she was, she didn't get very big; her mother only thought that she was gaining weight. During the nine months of pregnancy, the girl only thought she was sick. Her parents later discovered what had happened. They owned a small grocery store attached to the house and hired a young boy, about age fifteen, to help them with the shop. He spent a lot of time in the store and around the house. One winter day, the parents were away or busy in the shop when the boy went inside the house to warm up as it was very cold. The girl was at home, too, so they cuddled together on the heated *ondol* floor beneath a blanket, trying to keep warm. To entertain themselves, they "played" under the blanket, not understanding that their play was sex, and what could happen as the result.

I asked the newspapers to report on our program because I strongly believed that adoption included the birth mother, and we had to do something to help them too. So I asked the newspapers to help us spread the word about our program. They refused. This was 1969, and the papers of the time did not talk of such things on their pages. Only the tabloids mentioned such things. The reputable papers refused to discuss unwed mothers, not wanting to bring attention to such an embarrassing and shameful subject. I thought: now what am I going to do? No newspapers even wanted to talk about adoption because who wants to think about that? Nobody, they said. Besides, they told me, adoption must be a confidential matter, a private affair, and to write about it in the paper would frighten many people who did not want to reveal themselves as adoptive parents or birth parents who abandoned their children. But our program could save children's lives, I said. We want unwed mothers to know about us so we can help them, I said. The newspaper editors and reporters did not agree.

CAPOK's plan in Korea was to train Korean social workers well enough so that Koreans eventually could run the agency themselves, and the Christian Reformed Mission would then withdraw. That's when I became director, in 1971.

Around this same time, I got a phone call from Myung Soo Chang, a senior writer at *Jung-Ang Daily* newspaper (she later became the president of *Hangook Ilbo* and quite famous). She had gone to Ewha University as I did, and was two years my junior. Although I did not know her then (she was a journalism major), she knew me because I was the president of the student body. When she learned that I was working at an adoption agency, she called and left a message for me to ask if she could do an interview for an article in her newspaper. I was in the United States at that time, but when I returned we met and she wrote the article the others would not; she wrote about Korean adoption and our unwed mothers program. She also introduced me to all the most distinguished senior reporters of the most prestigious daily newspapers of Korea, and at some point they all wrote articles on this subject.

All of a sudden, all the other newspapers started calling, asking for interviews. All of those reporters were Ms. Chang's friends, and she helped us by convincing them of the importance of our story so that they would do as she had done and write about our services. Full-length stories ran in all those newspapers and brought us the publicity we needed to expand our programs. From then on, we had more media attention than we could handle. The newspapers and magazines and television producers came knocking on our doors, begging for interviews and more statistics about unwed mothers. We had created a buzz, and unwed mothers became a hot news topic.

In 1971, I helped start the unwed mothers group home still known as Ae Ran Won. Back then, the home was a fledgling program claiming to do "rehabilitation" for prostitutes. When I met the director, who also had gone to Ewha University (a year younger than me), the program was failing because the girls kept running away. The problem was that these girls had been living on the streets, and the police had caught them and put them in the shelter; the girls had not come voluntarily, and so they did not stay. There was no way to lock the girls in at night, and talking to them and praying for them didn't seem to help, the director told me. I told her that the next time she had an advisory board meeting, I would come to speak and suggest a new idea. Twice I spoke and convinced them to close down Ae Ran Won as a "rehabilitation" center and reopen as a real unwed mothers group home. They tried it and it worked. The girls stopped running away; they came on their own. The social workers got proper training, and soon Ae Ran Won became a model for other homes in Korea.

Eventually, the unwed mother stories and media attention brought us so much publicity that we were able to hold big fundraisers, like the Korean Benefit Dinner. That was something we started in Korea, and an idea I brought with me later to America. For our dinner in Korea, someone suggested that we ask the then-famous singer, Patty Kim, to perform. I didn't know how to contact her, but my assistant had a friend who had married a producer at KBS-TV who knew Patty Kim, and the superstar singer said yes. We couldn't pay her a penny but she agreed to do it for free. Two years later we had television producers and stars' agents asking us if they could perform at our next benefit dinner.

In time, we were choosing which magazines and newspapers we would give interviews to, thanks to my old college friend, Ms. Chang. I have heard that the agencies now have to pay for media coverage; there are too many unwed mother stories and the media has lost interest.

I became well-known in and outside of adoption circles and came to meet key government officials like the bureau chief of the Women and Child Welfare Department. Ms. Kim always listened to me. I visited her at her office every month and we talked about the latest adoption issues. Around 1973, she asked me to help her push for a new government adoption policy. "Your agency is proving that in-country adoptions are working," she said. "Nobody ever believed this would work before. I want to make this a policy of the government." And she did. That same year, the Korean government created a quota system for in-country adoptions. To begin with, ten percent of all adoptions had to be in-country and they planned to raise that percentage every year. Ms. Kim hoped to increase in-country adoptions enough to stop international adoptions altogether by 1988, but she retired before then.

CAPOK grew to a fairly large agency, with 300 to 500 foster homes and an unwed mothers counseling program, as well as in-country adoption. Adoptions rose to about 200 per year. We opened a branch in Taegu. In the mid-seventies, we moved out of the dingy old quarters at the Old Severance Hospital building and relocated to a building we shared with Holt. Originally, we owned the building and rented out a few floors to Holt, but soon the arrangement became a problem. There were two adoption agencies in the same building competing for the limited number of Korean families who were willing to do in-country adoptions. Holt had to make as many in-country placements as possible, because the government made it mandatory in 1973 that some proportion of all adoptions must be domestic. CAPOK, on the other hand, only did domestic Korean adoptions, but had more limited funds and resources to find families. Holt had more funding due to the international adoptions they did. To make a long story short, it was decided that my agency would merge with the Holt agency, especially because I knew that I was going to go to America. We did that merger six months before I left, and Holt took over the building and our agency.

Before I left for America in 1975, there were approximately five thousand in-country adoptions per year—recorded adoptions, that is. That number hasn't changed much, maybe it's increased to seven thousand, but I think there may be as many as ten or fifteen thousand—if you count the unrecorded adoptions.

One last step before I could move my family to America was to get permission from the Korean government. Quietly, I submitted my paperwork, not wanting the bureau chief of Women and Children, Ms. Kim, to find out that I was leaving her. I was afraid that she would not want me to go, for I had done much to help Korean adoptions. My fears were not completely unfounded. When Ms. Kim finally found out that I was leaving for America (too late for her to stop it), she was upset. "Why are you leaving?" she said. "What are you going to do about in-country adoptions?" I told her that Holt would continue my work. She said, "No, you must do it; you cannot leave. Had I known about this, I wouldn't have let you go."

I didn't think I would ever make it to America, but then the director of the American agency hand-delivered my papers on the U.S. side, so I was approved for a visa in three months. My husband and I sold our house in Korea, and on June 15, 1975, I moved to America and became a social worker for Children's Home Society of Minnesota (CHSM).

My daughter was twelve and my son five when I was preparing to move to America and take a new job. I had to go to the U.S. Embassy to get a visa. The official interviewed my husband first, and after a very short time my husband came out with a big smile, showing me his visa stamp. Then it was my turn, and the official asked me how I could work at the American adoption agency as a social worker. I said "Why not?" He smiled and said that I was the first person he had ever heard of who was going to the United States to become a social worker. After several more questions about my adoption work experience he looked quite impressed. Then, all of a sudden, he asked "Is your son your birth son?" My immediate answer, without thinking about it, was going to be "No, we adopted him," but God helped me with a few seconds to think and I said "Yes." Like all other Korean parents, we registered our son as a birth son on our legal documents.

My heart stopped. I waited. My imagination ran wild as I tried to figure out why the consulate was so interested in my son, and why they were questioning my husband separately, and why they hadn't asked him about our son. I thought maybe they are suspicious of me because I am the person who was offered the job that made it possible for us to move to America; maybe they didn't believe that I had been offered a job as a social worker. The year was 1975; this sort of thing was not common. Did the consulate think I was faking my employment? Finally, the official smiled at me and said everything was okay; we could go to America. I found out later that the official had kept me in an unusually long interview not because he was questioning the legitimacy of my son but because he wanted to know more about me. He wondered what kind of Korean woman an American agency would want to hire to be a social worker.

Social Work ~ America

My annual salary my first year in America was less than I had been earning in Korea. Can you believe it? We shouldn't have moved, given up our house and land in Korea (which I later learned was worth millions) just to come to America, but the decision was not mine. My husband wanted to become an American citizen.

You see, I married a North Korean man who had to leave his home, his country and his family because of the war. That meant that some day, he would want to go back. The signing of the armistice in 1953 was the signing of my husband's unfortunate fate. He no longer had a place to call home. In his mind, South Korea was a temporary home for him. Later, during the war, he discovered that being an American could be his ticket north, back to his first and only home.

"*Yobo*, Americans have special rights," my husband said. "Their government protects the American citizens forever. Wherever they go overseas for jobs they make ten times more than a Korean makes. They are also safe from war. No other country can invade America."

How could I refuse? He had a better chance of visiting North Korea if he was an American citizen than if he was South Korean. All along, this was his plan, and I had no idea he was thinking such thoughts. When I was given the opportunity to visit America for a four-month social work program, I didn't know that my husband's secret American dream moved from the realm of wishful thinking to our family's reality. And then I remembered what a fortune teller had told my mother many years ago. She told my mother that in the future I was going to live overseas. I was thirteen or so when my mother told me what the fortune teller had said, and of course I didn't believe her. I knew nothing about America and had just seen Americans for the first time during the war, only a year or two before. But the fortune teller insisted and ended up being right. My husband had a plan, and I had become his ticket—via America—back to his northern home.

I first came to the United States in 1971 as part of the Twin Cities International Program (TCIP), which was an international exchange of ideas for social workers and teachers. During my four-month stay I was placed with different host families, and these people were my first contact with American life and culture.

Before the TCIP began, the Christian Adoption Program of Korea (CAPOK) had asked me to go a month early and visit Michigan (home of the Christian Reformed Church) and Colorado to talk about the Korean adoption programs. I flew to Colorado first via New York, and I barely remember my very first overseas flight because I had taken a lot of medication for motion sickness and was completely out of it. My escorts were an elderly retired couple, Mr. and Mrs. Hubers. He was the former CEO of Christian Reformed Korean Mission (CRKM), and CAPOK was under CRKM but licensed as an independent adoption agency. They greeted me in Colorado at the airport and were my hosts during my visit. Imagine my surprise when we arrived at their house. I stared: a giant car-home? Can you believe it? That was the first time I had ever seen a luxury mobile home. Later, they took me to their daughter's home for a tour of a regular American home and I could not believe that they had so many televisions—even in the children's room—and a bathroom with a shower for each bedroom. Later I learned that the daughter's husband was in the construction business and they were considered very rich by American standards, not just by my Korean ones.

After Colorado I went to Grand Rapids, Michigan, and stayed at the mission CEO's home. Unfortunately, I had gotten sick and developed a very violent cough. I thought I was going to die. I kept the entire family up at night with my coughing fits. To help me, the family turned their home into a steam room. That cured my cough after about three days but made the whole house damp-wet. They didn't mind, though; they wanted to be sure I could deliver my speech.

The director and his family were devout Christians. I was impressed that they prayed before each meal, and after every meal they read a paragraph from the Bible. This was their custom at every single meal. Can you believe that? So when the director's daughter came to visit and brought her baby, I was surprised by her seemingly non-Christian ways, at least compared to Korean ways. The baby was crying, as babies do, but instead of soothing the baby's cries, the daughter put the baby in another room in a crib and closed the door. She came out to the dining room and sat down with the rest of us and everyone talked and laughed and ate. Meanwhile, the baby continued to scream. "Hyun Sook, aren't you hungry?" someone asked. I nodded my head no. How could I eat? How could all of them eat while the baby cried and cried and cried? In Korea, a good parent never leaves a small baby—any child under age one or two—alone and crying, I thought. Good Korean parents would hold the baby and comfort him or let him fall asleep in their arms until he went to sleep naturally, even during meal time; a baby cannot be forced to sleep. During that lunch, I sat quietly and angrily thinking of that young woman: you cannot be a good mother. Later I learned about naptime and that in America it was okay to put the baby down alone; he would cry himself to sleep eventually.

On this trip, I also saw my very first computer. There were no small personal computers at this time; they were big mainframes. One of the men from the church who showed me around the city was vice president of a computer company and he took me on a tour of his company. I didn't understand them at all, but I was amazed. (Even today, I don't understand computers; I only use mine for email.) This same man invited me to his church congregation dinner with his family; he had six children. I remember that he said grace before the meal, but he forgot the last part: in Jesus' name we pray. That was the cue that the prayer was ending, and we could say Amen. He didn't say it, though. We waited and waited with our heads bowed, wondering what to do and finally one of his children whispered the words to him. Everybody laughed. I guess he was so excited about the dinner that he forgot.

That was my first month in America. In April, I headed for Minnesota to begin the TCIP. Up until then, my destinations had been warm enough for me to wear the light raincoat I had brought from Korea. When I got to Minnesota, it was raining and snowing and freezing cold. I called my husband in Korea: "I am dying, Husband; I'm freezing to death!" He told me he had wired money to me and to go buy a winter coat. I spent almost three weeks picking one out because they seemed so expensive to me, and I felt bad spending so much money on myself for just a coat. Finally, I picked out a leather jacket only to discover later that although I had bought a quality jacket, it was not real leather. I was so disappointed. However, the jacket was of good quality and in fact, I still have it now. My sister wears it; only the lining has been replaced in thirty years. Now, I don't feel so bad about the cost.

My first TCIP host family was a Caucasian husband and Chinese wife. They wrote to me before I arrived so I could learn about them a little. The husband was a lawyer and said that his wife was a dancer. However, the wife preferred to describe herself as a ballet teacher. She worried that I might misunderstand the word "dancer" and think she was an exotic dancer. The wife looked like a ballet teacher with her long, straight black hair, which she sometimes tucked into a ponytail.

I had a hard time at first with this family. They gave me my own room and showed me around the house, explaining where to find everything. In the kitchen, the wife opened up the pantry and refrigerator and told me to eat whatever I wanted: there was nothing but a few carrots and some lettuce. I remembered that my lunches were free as part of the program; during the day, I attended classes; the wife said she would provide dinner. The next morning I went into the kitchen to try to find something to make for breakfast but there was nothing, not even eggs. I wasn't about to eat celery or carrots for breakfast, so I went to my classes and was starving until lunchtime. Imagine my disappointment when I saw that there were only sandwiches for lunch. In Korea, that is just a snack. I needed a warm meal.

I called my husband in Korea: "Yobo, I am starving! I have nothing to eat!" He told me to use the money he had sent me and buy some groceries. He was not happy that his wife had $2,000 in the bank but was starving instead of buying food. The problem was that I was used to Korean foods: soups, rice, meat and side dishes. I knew that I couldn't find those same foods in an American grocery store, so the wife took me to a Chinese grocery store and I was able to buy some ramen noodle soup mix. Oh, I ate ramen with eggs every single morning for the next two weeks. Ramen, ramen, ramen. I even got the wife to try the noodles, and she eventually ate them for breakfast, too. But that was not the end of my food troubles with this host family.

Another time, the next-door neighbor invited us to dinner. I looked forward to visiting and eating with new people. My mistake: I thought dinner was at six-thirty. We did not go until seven-thirty, and when we got there they did not serve dinner right away. They served us drinks. I didn't drink and I was tired from being in class all day and straining to follow American English all day long, that everyone spoke so fast. I was starving. Finally, we ate, but it was after 8:30 p.m. After that, whenever we were invited for dinner someplace, I made sure I ate something beforehand. You see, Koreans have a set meal time and they sit down and eat right away; they talk after, not before. I was not used to the American customs.

I went to church with the husband a few times. He knew I liked church and invited me to come along with him. His wife, however, didn't attend, so he usually went alone. Most of the congregation at his church knew he had an "Oriental" wife but they had never met her, so when I showed up a few Sundays at his side, they mistook me for his wife. He explained that I was their guest and called me his "host child" and said he was the "host father," which was really funny to me because he was younger than me, twenty-nine, and I was thirty-one or thirty-two.

My second host family lived near Lake of the Isles, a neighborhood in Minneapolis not far from my first host family's home. The house was like a palace. I lived with the mother and her four children. She was divorced. Her ex-

husband owned a factory and was quite wealthy, so I think
he left her and the children the house. One of the girls gave
up her room to me and bunked with her sister, so I had a
room to myself again. The family had a big dog, which I was
not used to, and he usually slept in the girl's room that I now
occupied. Even though the girls brought the dog to bed with
them in the other room, in the middle of the night the dog
came back into the room I now slept in, mistaking it for his
room, and jumped up on my bed. I was scared to death and
couldn't sleep that first night. The next day I couldn't bring
myself to tell the mother what happened because I was
embarrassed to be afraid of a dog, but I didn't want that dog
in my room again. That next night, I took everything I could
move or lift in the bedroom and shoved it up against the
door to keep the dog out. No one ever knew.

The first morning I went into the kitchen for breakfast,
I knew I was going to be hungry again. This family ate cereal
and milk for breakfast, every morning. Cereal and milk.
Cereal and milk. I didn't drink milk; that wasn't common in
Korea then. And cereal wasn't a real breakfast to me; I was
used to a hot meal to start the day, so again, I left for class
starving until lunchtime. Fortunately, by the third week I felt
better. The mother made good dinners every night for the
children, so I ate well then—except for Fridays. They were
Jewish and served kosher lamb Friday nights. I didn't know
what kosher was or what seasonings they used, I just knew it
smelled very bad to me. I had never had lamb nor smelled
any meat made that way. The odors made me sick. Ironically,
I later grew to like lamb and I often order it when I am
invited to a nice restaurant.

This host mother was the first divorced woman I had
ever met. I had a hard time understanding her family life; it

was so different from Korea, but I liked her very much. She was easy to talk to, so I asked many questions and learned many things about different American families. For instance, a divorced woman could have a boyfriend. Every weekend, this lady's boyfriend came to the house and had dinner with all of us, including the children. I remember he brought roses; later, I heard that they got married. In Korea, this would have been strange. No Korean man would ever marry a divorced woman, especially one with four children from her previous husband. Another custom that surprised me was that the ex-husband came by the house some Fridays and picked up the children to go on an outing. I didn't understand this sharing. When Koreans divorce, the husband is solely responsible for the children unless he abandons them. The children are the husband's, not the wife's. I asked my host mother how she provided for her children. She explained that her husband gave her money, alimony, and gave her more money for the children, child support. Oh, gee, I thought. Americans have such a different family life. She went on to explain that if she remarried then her husband would stop paying the alimony but would continue to pay child support. All of that was so hard for me to understand. Up until then, I had only met families with no divorces. Now, here I was in America watching some man visit this woman and her children, carrying a bouquet of flowers. Women were much luckier in America than in Korea. More chances.

I gave this host mother one of my nicest Korean dresses. I had brought the green silk dress for special TCIP events. Program officials also told me to bring gifts for my host families, so I brought beautiful shawls and stones to be made into jewelry and many other gifts for all of my host families.

One day, I was wearing my green silk dress for some occasion when this host mother saw me and said: "Oh! You look so cute! That dress is so beautiful!" I turned to her and said, "Okay, you like it? You can have it. It's yours." She said no, but I insisted. That was the Korean way.

At the end of my second host family stay, TCIP hosted a special party for all of the program participants and their host families. I think there were almost thirty participants from various countries. We had to introduce ourselves, so I stood up and said: "My name is Hyun Sook Shim. I am from Korea. I am the mother of one child; my daughter is seven. I am a social worker at such-and-such agency. I have been starving at my host families' homes. I hope my third family will feed me."

That was my way of joking, but at the same time, I had hoped my third host family would hear me. They didn't; my host mother was late to the party. When she finally came, a lady with the thickest eyeglasses, she found me and was told, jokingly, by the others that I was "starving in the mornings" so she had better feed me well. This lady asked me what I was used to eating in Korea, and I told her: rice and kimchi and other side dishes and soups. Do you know what? She got up every morning and made me Minute Rice herself. Now, this woman's husband was president of a garment company and they had a nice home in Highland Park in St. Paul; they even had an English housemaid who did not like that the wife cooked me rice every morning herself. Their daughter was in college and their son was still at home, going to high school. So it was a big deal that this lady made me rice each morning, even if it was Minute Rice, which I had never had before and did not like very much. What I really loved about this family was the beautiful gardens the wife kept. In fact, many people came on tours to see her flower and vegetable gardens.

Although I was able to eat rice daily now, there still was no way to buy kimchi at this time in Minnesota. There were no Korean grocery stores, so I discovered that dill pickles were the closest thing to kimchi I could find. A jar was ninety-nine cents, which was expensive to me, and unfortunately, I had a jar-a-day habit. My host mother thought my habit was very funny and told all her friends about my rice-and-pickle diet. She was a very social person, with a great interest in other cultures, and I gave her a lot to tell her lady friends.

We had a few misunderstandings about cars one time. Her car was dirty so I asked her if I could wash it for her. She told me absolutely not. I didn't understand why she wouldn't let me wash her car for her, so one day while she was busy doing something, I went outside with water and a sponge and started washing the car. She found me before I finished and ended up taking it to the car wash herself. Our other car confusion had to do with her husband. Remember, he was president of his company. I thought it strange that he drove the Oldsmobile and his wife drove the nice convertible Cadillac. I said to him: "In Korea, you would have a professional driver to drive for you all the time." He asked why. I said, "Because the president of a company would never drive himself." He laughed and explained that in America, most people drive themselves unless they are President of the United States or a famous person, but company presidents didn't need drivers. Even some governors drive themselves, he said. That surprised me. I still believed that he should have the nicer car and a driver, but I was learning that in America, things were different.

After a week or so, the wife asked me if I would like to continue to stay with them or move into my own apartment. She wanted me to stay, but the program was offering the participants an opportunity to share some apartments for part of their stay. Do you know what happened? Only two or three of the girls from Asia stayed with their host families; the rest, about ninety-five percent, moved into the apartments. I guess all of us were starving, ha, ha! No, really, American culture was hard for us to adjust to and understand. I turned down the offer and stayed with my host family for one more month. The idea of living in an apartment on my own, or even with a roommate, scared me to death. In Korea, a young woman would never live alone in an apartment, and she definitely would not do that in a strange country. My stay with that family was cut short, though, because their house in Highland Park was too far away from my new assignment for the last part of the program, which was at Children's Home Society of Minnesota (CHSM).

Even after I moved, I still visited my host mother in Highland Park on weekends because I enjoyed her company and she was very nice to me. She introduced me to the good American life, although I was too young to appreciate it properly; I took her lifestyle for granted. Like her fancy houseboat; she took it out on the Mississippi River some weekends but I didn't really appreciate it enough because I wasn't used to it. Now, I wish I had that kind of opportunity more often. This host mother also took me to fancy restaurants and let me order prime rib, which I loved at the time. Those were some of the best meals I ever had. When I returned to America to become a permanent resident later, nobody took me out for prime rib dinners. The husband also gave me lots of clothing and coats and jackets from his garment company for my family in Korea. I received gifts that came from places they traveled like England and France. I was very spoiled.

CHSM arranged for me to stay with one of their supervisors and her husband in their house near the CHSM offices. This woman and her husband also were very good to me. They gave me rides everywhere and invited me to their cabin in Wisconsin, which was like a dream with the woods and lake. I had such a good time with them.

As part of my program training, I went to Duluth, Minnesota, to meet other social workers and learn about the American way of doing home visits. I stayed with a family that weekend and discovered that not everyone had air conditioning. I didn't know that. Every other house I had been in had it. That weekend, I learned that not all Americans were rich.

I worked very hard those last couple of weeks of the program. I was having fun learning about American culture and learning everything I could about American adoption agencies, so that I could bring what I learned back to Korea. Roger Toogood was the executive director of CHSM then, and he let me spend a lot of time with him, learning all the ropes. I went to United Way meetings, learned about fundraising and budgeting, went on home visits and so on. I worked nights and weekends, trying to absorb everything. After two months at this pace, I ended up fainting one day from a lack of sleep.

One day, Mr. Toogood came to me and in a very serious voice said, "You didn't tell us the truth; you've been lying to us." What, I thought. I never lied, I told him, wondering what he was talking about and afraid that I had done something very wrong. He smiled. "It's your birthday today!" he said. "Why didn't you tell us?" You see, he was referring to my legal birth date. I had to explain to him about my true birthday being a completely different date, in February, not the legal date of June 15.

One last TCIP story: an adoption program supervisor from CHSM invited me and another social worker who was Filipino (and from the same TCIP group) to her home in Lake City, Minnesota, for a fun weekend. We made fondue, which was so fun for me. Our hostess had made a lot of American dishes but she also made rice for us, knowing that we liked it. She brought out a regular-sized bowl of rice at first, and we waited for her to bring out more bowls, thinking that one bowl was only enough for one person. Meanwhile, this lady sat down and began eating; we realized she was not going to bring out any more rice. I said, "What do we do with one bowl of rice?" She explained that it was for all of us to share. I looked at the Filipino social worker. Our hostess said, "You need more rice?" We both nodded our heads and said, "Yes! Three times more!" We all laughed. She realized her mistake and promised to make us more rice next time. She taught us about American fondue; we taught her about the proper amount of rice to serve when you have Asian guests.

At CHSM, I felt that the entire staff really liked me, and they really helped me. I learned a lot that I could use in my work in Korea for the next five years, up until I moved to the United States. For example, I used the U.S. concepts and ways of thinking about adoption, and the new idea of post-adoption services. I especially developed the ideas I learned from Mrs. Marietta Spencer's teachings and workshops. Also, while back in Korea, I did a lot to help CHSM connect with Korean adoption agencies.

That was my first time in America, through the TCIP. Aside from work, I was able to do a lot of shopping and ended up spending all the money my husband had given me for my trip. Unfortunately, not everything I bought was very nice. I didn't know what I was buying, so I ended up buying a lot of junk and paying too much for it. My husband wasn't mad, though; he understood that it was my first time overseas. He wanted me to have fun. I felt bad for wasting all that money.

When it was time to return to Korea I felt so sad, but at the same time I was very anxious to go back home and see my daughter, whom I had left with my husband and a housemaid. I could not stay longer than four months with my daughter at home, but I did make one final stop before returning to Korea: Disneyland. I flew to Los Angeles en route to Korea and visited the famous amusement park. With the last of my money, I bought a ticket and spent a hot August afternoon trying to see everything but, finally, I was unable to tour the entire park.

Children's Home Society of Minnesota

Imagine a Korean woman with her husband and two young children. The woman, at her husband's urging and lifelong dream, has taken a job in America as a social worker. She has agreed to continue her work in Korean adoptions in Minnesota while helping her family settle into their new home, but to do that she has had to sell her home and land in Korea and bid farewell to her family and friends. In exchange, she will take on a new language, always speaking it first, work side-by-side with people whose customs she does not understand, learn a new work culture, live a different life and watch herself slowly release, one by one, the ties to her other life, her other country, her other self.

I became a social worker for CHSM in 1975. The first days were made easier with the kindness of my former host family, my co-workers and the executive director, Mr. Roger Toogood. My Highland Park host mother from my TCIP days had found an apartment for me and my family to rent. The building was within walking distance of CHSM's St. Paul offices. I walked around our apartment and inspected everything. When I opened up the refrigerator, I was amazed and surprised: it was filled with food. Can you imagine? There was fruit, meat, cheese and jars of pickles. I never expected such a thing; we didn't have to grocery shop for weeks. My former host mother had thought of everything. Mr. Toogood met us at the airport and helped us move all of our belongings into our new home. I liked to joke with him that if he hadn't hired me, I would have stayed in Korea and become rich and successful. Of course, in America, I had become very rich and successful in a different way.

When I started at CHSM, my office was not ready so I shared an office with my supervisor for a while. I didn't mind sharing the small office space as my supervisor worked in the St. Paul office only three days a week, as she spent the other part of her week in southern Minnesota. We had a good arrangement and got along; in fact, both of us were talkers and quite loud. I always knew when she was in the office; I could hear her in the hall. "Good morning!" she often shouted. "How are you?" She laughed loud, too, like I do myself.

We each had our own desks and supplies, and I always respected her space, even when she was not there. But all of a sudden, she began to lose things. In her loud voice, she would announce: "Where are my rulers? Who has my erasers? Did somebody take my pen?" She never seemed to direct these questions at me but I was the only one sharing her office; I worried that everyone else had heard her. I became scared. I was new, I was Korean, and I was trying to fit in with my new co-workers. I thought she was accusing me of stealing, and I didn't know what to say or do. Meanwhile, many other social workers in the building began to report that they were missing money from their purses. I carried a lot of cash, because I was accustomed to carrying at least one hundred dollars at all times in Korea. Like the others, I also began to notice that money had disappeared from my purse during the work day, but I didn't tell anyone. I was afraid that no one would believe me. Worse yet, I was afraid that everyone blamed me, and so I kept silent. Several months later, the matter had been resolved and the culprit caught. An employee had been caught stealing from the petty cash box, and that led to the discovery that she also was responsible for the thefts from people's purses and desks. But I was not yet relieved. I had lost quite a bit of money and finally spoke up.

"Why didn't you say anything?" my supervisor asked.

"Why?" I said. "Well, because you always complained that someone stole your ruler and your pens and everything. I thought you were talking about me. I thought you were accusing me."

She looked at me in disbelief. "Hyun Sook, are you serious?" she said. "Did I really make you feel that bad?"

"You were talking as if I were the thief," I said.

She shook her head. "No, no, I wasn't accusing you of stealing," she said. "I was only joking, talking like that. I didn't think you would take me seriously. How could you think such a thing of me?"

"How am I supposed to know?" I said. "I just moved here. How can I understand you? You talk so loud and blunt; I thought that meant you were serious."

"Oh, Hyun Sook," she said. "I am so sorry. You misunderstood. That is how we joke; that is American culture. No one believed you were the thief; they all knew I was joking. Except you."

She felt so bad about that mix-up. We both learned about each other's cultures that day, and I realized I had a lot to learn about the American sense of humor. Many many years later, quite a few of my American friends told me that I am just like my office mate.

My first year at CHSM was hell. Every day was stressful because I was learning. I was not used to American ways, especially not American English. Although I spoke English, I was not used to communicating in it all day long at work. Trying to keep up with a group conversation was especially challenging for me. You see, I led small group discussions back then. I was fine one-on-one but struggled to understand group discussions when more than one person at a time spoke. On top of that, many of the participants were smokers, and I remember feeling like I was stuck in a chimney. All that smoke made me very lightheaded. You see, people were allowed to smoke indoors then. When smoking was banned indoors, I was so happy. What kept me going in those days were the same people who sometimes confused me and drove me crazy; they were good people and I really liked them. In fact, I still keep in touch with many of the adoptive parents and staff from those days.

Those were also the days when adoptive parents respected social workers; the parents looked to us for guidance and help. I'm not saying that today parents don't respect us; it's just a different sort of respect now. Back then, many social workers were much older than me and had many more years of experience. Several also were adoptive parents themselves, like me; like Mr. Toogood. For us back then, adoption was a very personal experience which had become a very personal vocation. We had passion for our work. Communication and relationships with the adoptive parents were very important to us. After all these years, I feel like I have at least something—one thing—useful to share.

My career at CHSM was good to me. I excelled and did what I could for all those families and their children. My passion kept me from taking any supervisory positions; I didn't want to delegate. I liked getting involved with children and families. I love to be close to and "touch" the lives of the people we help. One of my great blessings is that I have held and been close physically and spiritually to thousands of children. I have been there at the beginning, seen them grow into college graduates, become wives and husbands. I have counseled, laughed and cried with them and their parents. I always believed I worked for the children and parents, and that was what I was best at. Administrative work was not what I would have been best at. I had a promise to fulfill.

Over the years, I placed hundreds and hundreds of children. Now that I am older and hopefully a little wiser, I can look back and say that not all of them were successful. In fact, a few of my cases still haunt me; I still feel some guilt.

If a parent wanted a healthy baby, I always placed a healthy baby. Or so I thought. How could I always know back then? Sometimes there weren't good medical records kept in Korea, and even medical tests in America didn't show everything. We didn't always know what to test for. I remember one case in which a very young baby girl I placed turned out to have a severe case of cerebral palsy; she also had some serious developmental disabilities. You know what?

The parents never complained; they never told me what had happened as the child grew older. I saw them again later—when they came to apply for their second child. This time, they asked for a healthy boy. That's when I found out about that first placement. The parents had hired a full-time caretaker to help them with their daughter. I don't think they blamed me but I felt forever guilty. Those were the early days when we placed infants as young as two-and-a-half months with limited medical histories and tests. Back then, we just didn't know as much.

Other placements end up changing a parent's life in amazing ways. One Minnesota family adopted an apparently healthy and normal little girl, but then discovered that she had CP and other potentially serious problems. With many surgeries and a lot of treatment, she later was able to walk independently. I'm eternally grateful for her parents. They said, "We are so thankful to have our daughter. We have health insurance for her, and we could open our eyes to appreciate her culture, and we've made so many good friends among other adoptive parents. It wouldn't have happened if we did not adopt her." Other parents of CP children have become dedicated professionals in the field of special needs children. Those are the stories that help ease the pain of the less successful placements.

One of the biggest challenges I have seen in the placement of children has to do with the ones who are adopted when they are older. I think that children who are older than two years may face challenges later. People may expect some attachment issues in addition to any other types of problems we might anticipate. I remember all those little children in the snow banks during the war. Still, some general problems are often just the result of a child's particular personality, not necessarily adoption. Birth children may bond differently (or not at all) with their birth parents. Look at me and my siblings; I bonded with my mother in a different way compared to some of my younger siblings, even though I was not adopted. How do you explain that? I think there are just different levels of attachment and different kinds of relationships.

There are some troubling stories, though. I remember one placement of mine. The child was adopted from an Eastern European country when she was between eleven and thirteen months old. You wouldn't think that's old enough to cause such difficult behavior problems when she got older, but when she became a teenager, trouble began. This girl ran away a lot. The parents tried everything, looking for help and taking advantage of all possible resources, but nothing worked. I think she had a dislocated hip when I placed her; she had surgeries when she was young. Physically, she healed but emotionally, she seemed to fall apart as she got older. Sometimes, we just cannot know what happened to a child between her birth and the time she was brought to an orphanage and placed for adoption, no matter how old or young. These kinds of stories trouble me. All those years ago, I kept placing child after child, never knowing what happened to them after they were adopted, not finding out about the after-effects until, sometimes, it was too late to help. No one ever came back to me wanting to return a child. No one ever called up to complain. How could I know what was happening back then? But these stories demonstrate to me how much the parents are dedicated to the welfare of their children, and how much they love them.

One girl I placed was diagnosed with bipolar disorder when she was thirteen. When the psychiatrist told me this,

I worried that she would struggle for the rest of her life. Many years later I saw her and could not believe my eyes. She was married and a mother herself. I said to her: "Is that you?" She replied, "Yes, it's me! I know I was hopeless back then but now I'm so much better." She made me so happy. I thought she was lost back then, and now I saw that she had found herself.

Some parents wanted to adopt a third or fourth or fifth child, and sometimes I was against this. If they were adopting children who had been raised in orphanages, I knew there might be behavioral problems as the children got older. With too many children in a family with problems, I knew that would be hard both for the parents and for the children. Difficult children changed a family dynamic. I'm not saying that some of these children grew up to be criminals or have real serious problems, but some behavioral issues are long term and hard for parents and children. Those types of problems were not simply stages— like being a teenager; those were for real; those were forever. As I am a parent myself, I know how a parent worries about their children.

When placing a child with a family, I tried hard to make sure the couple was stable. Of course, who can know who will divorce? We cannot predict the future. There is no such thing as a perfect couple (although, luckily, I met many who came close!), but I tried very hard to figure out who would be good parents. If I saw that at least one parent was strong, dedicated and a loving person, I approved the adoption. My belief was that if at least one parent was strong and stable, then the adoption (if not always the marriage) would work. That child would be loved. For example, I remember one couple who divorced years after adopting. The wife was the kind of person who didn't like to leave their child with a babysitter. If she and her husband went out together, she would have to call home dozens of times. Eventually, the couple divorced. They came back to CHSM many years later for a workshop, and at that time, I did not know they had divorced. When I found out, I asked them why they came together by airplane from another state. They told me: "This workshop is important to both of us to attend. When it comes to our Korean-born child, we act together—as parents—despite our divorce." They showed me a new side to parents' dedication. I love parents like them and have such great respect for them.

Some adopted children, as they grow older and more independent, often become angry with their adoptive parents, just because they are the parents. Some of those children, once they are adults, find and meet their birth parents and then become estranged from their adoptive parents. When the adult adoptees are angry, they sometimes blame their adoptive parents. And then they hate their birth parents. Back and forth, back and forth. That is very hard, for both parent and child. Me, I am an adoptive mother, too, and when I see this happen in families, I think of my own son.

One of my best successes was a Korean adoptee I placed as a child and later, when she was an adult, I helped her find her birth family. I think she was single when this happened. She brought her adoptive parents with her to meet her birth parents, then she took her husband to meet her birth mother and later, she took her first child to meet her Korean family. Nowadays, she doesn't visit as often because she is so busy raising her children (she later adopted another child), but she keeps in touch with her birth mother. To me, this is the kind of relationship I hope all adoptees who have found their birth parents can have with their adoptive and birth parents, to be close to both and show love and respect for both. That is what I hope for every family.

But I must also confess to the times I got in trouble. I have always been strong-willed, and ready to say what I think. Combine that with my sometimes broken English, and people can think that I am blunt and insensitive in a way that I never intended. Because of that tendency, I learned that a few adoptive parents in the past did not want to work with me. That has been one of my great career hurts—and regrets.

In one case, maybe ten years ago, I was working with an adoptive couple and suggested that if the woman would lose some weight, then they could meet Korea's weight criteria. Back then, Korea didn't always allow people who were overweight to adopt; they considered it a health risk. I also knew that this couple was concerned about the cost of international adoption, so I told them how some people borrow money from their parents to adopt. I also told them of other methods that people use to come up with the fees. This couple was very angry with me and wrote a letter of complaint to the agency president. They said that I discriminated against them because of their weight and financial status. I didn't intend to be understood that way. I was trying to help them. My blunt Korean ways seemed rude and disrespectful to them, when I thought I was offering helpful advice. You see, I have this mothering tendency. If I like someone, I can become quite pushy and straightforward. I do not mean it in a bad way; I am just trying to help the person.

Of course, professionally, I shouldn't do that. Other social workers have told me that my attitude was wrong. If I sense that a child with special needs is not the right fit for a particular couple, I don't feel it's right to approve their application just because they are willing to adopt and meet the basic criteria. I know this isn't a professional attitude; it's mine and I suppose it's rather Korean.

There was another family that I was working with who also asked to change social workers. At first I wondered if it was because they didn't want to work with a Korean social worker, but I knew they were adopting a Korean child, so I didn't think that could be it. I respected their wishes, but I was hurt. The couple wanted either an American infant or a Korean child. Initially, I suggested that they adopt an American infant; I thought they had a good chance to be chosen by an American birth mother for the adoption. I don't know what happened in that case. I guess it had to do with personality and cultural differences. My forever question.

Programs

During my years at CHSM, I helped start a number of programs. One of the first was the Korea Day Workshop, which was an informational session about Korea and Korean culture for adoptive parents. The workshop became a regular program because of all the adoptions we were doing then.

We also started the Teen Group in response to the growing need for continued post-adoption support to families who had adopted through us. This group was for the teens only, not their parents. We started it because some of the adoptees, especially the ones who were placed at a little older age from orphanages, were having problems. There were a lot of parents who didn't want to drive their kids back and forth so often for the meetings, so my colleague, Jeff Mondloh, had to transport them. Later, the kids wanted to eat Korean food so I cooked for them since there weren't any Korean restaurants yet. The first three or four years I cooked for them and cooked inexpensive meals, like the ones that would have been served in the orphanages or foster homes.

Not long after the Teen Group was up and running, we started a Pre-Teen Group because one of the adoptive mothers suggested that we teach kids about their heritage at an earlier age. At one point, I was working four nights a week in addition to full days.

Later, some of the children who had been adopted at an older age and remembered the orphanage asked why America didn't have a Children's Day like in Korea. They remembered that holiday because many visitors came to the orphanages with gifts, especially food, apples, candies and bread. They missed that celebration and asked why America didn't have one. I tried to joke with them and explain that America didn't have a Children's Day because every day is a child's day in America. They didn't laugh. So we started our annual Children's Day event, which grew and grew every year. We regularly changed the theme of the event and invited different panel speakers. My goal, before I retired, was to bring some Korean birth fathers to speak at the event for the older children and the parents. Unfortunately, the U.S. Embassy refused to grant visas for those men because they couldn't prove they had money or a job to return to in Korea. I was so disappointed that it was never possible to do this.

Three years after I started at CHSM, we began the Korean Benefit Dinner. The first year we raised $3,700. My goal was $37,000. Nobody thought we could do that, but we did eventually, until the event grew bigger than anyone imagined.

All of those programs still exist today; however, the Pre-Teen and Teen Groups have gotten smaller over the years as we place fewer Korean children. Also, there are so many other resources out there today that the need is not as great as when we started.

I was a workaholic in those days. I also made a lot of trips to and from Korea to try to foster communication between Korea and America and keep international adoptions at the forefront of discussions. I kept in touch with government officials, so that whenever there was talk of stopping adoptions, I could have my say. I pushed the agencies there to open up their records to us so we had background information on adopted children. They did, but when those adopted children returned as adults wanting to meet their birth parents, the Korean agencies closed their doors again. Now they do not provide that information at the time of referral. They only release it if we are conducting an official search.

Over the years, I developed and maintained relationships with the Korean media, agencies and government officials so that international adoptions would continue and Minnesota adoptions remained successful. I had a lot of help, too. CHSM always was behind me, supporting my efforts, and the adoptive parents were key players, too. Without them, we wouldn't have had all the volunteers we needed for all of our growing programs. With all that support, CHSM was able to develop the first post-adoption services in the country.

Accomplishments

In May 1987, I received an award from the president of Korea for my contributions to child welfare. Before arriving in Korea, I made a stop in Hong Kong and bought many gifts for all the people I would see, as this was the Korean custom. When I landed in Korea, I was running late for the award ceremony. Rushed, I took a taxi and put the gifts in the trunk. Can you guess what happened? I forgot to take the gifts out of the trunk when I got to the event. When I realized what had happened, I called that taxi company but the driver denied that there had been a large suitcase in his trunk. I was so angry with him and myself. Even if I had forgotten, he should have remembered. I had run out of money and couldn't buy replacement gifts, so it seemed as if I wasn't polite. How embarrassing.

Two years later, Governor Rudy Perpich dedicated a special day to me: Hyun Sook Han Day. However, this was a surprise to me. A month or so before the event, the staff asked me to attend an upcoming event with adopted Korean children, as they were going to invite some adoptive parents who would like to see me. I said fine and got the date for the event. Then they asked me if my husband would come, and two weeks before the event, they asked me if my daughter would come as well. I told them she could not get away from work. Finally, they asked me to wear my Korean dress. I thought: my *hanbok*? Why? To play with the children? I had no idea. Everyone surprised me. The parents and children came with balloons and cards, the Governor made his proclamation, I was presented with a beautiful gold necklace, and reporters covered the event for the local news. My husband was very proud. The biggest surprise of all was what was on stage hidden beneath a big cloth. I was asked to stand center stage as the surprise was unveiled: a portrait of me holding a child, surrounded by many others. One of the adoptive fathers had painted it from a photograph. I have it hanging in my house now, and it will be a treasure in my family forever. That whole event was something special that

I will always remember, so I give my sincere thanks to all the adoptive parents who made it happen.

In 1990, CHSM asked me for some personal background information and my resume. They were nominating me for the Child Welfare League of America's Outstanding Social Worker from the Midwest region. Roger Toogood, our director at that time, said that the Midwest had the most social workers so the competition was toughest in our region. Just to be nominated from Children's Home Society was an honor, so I really didn't know if I would win. One day, Mr. Toogood came running into my office and screamed: "You won! You've been chosen for the award!" I couldn't believe it. This was the first time a CHSM social worker had won the award, and it was a great honor. I got to go to Washington, D.C., to accept the award.

Children's Home has become so big now. When I first came here it was a small agency, but now it is many times larger. It has changed so much over the years, and always for the better. The most recent big change was when our current agency president, Madonna King, arrived after Roger Toogood retired. Two years after she came here, she said we needed to build a new building. The old building had many problems and needed to be torn down. We had two buildings, and my office was in the one that didn't need to be rebuilt, so I did not think this would affect me. By the third year she was here, Dr. King figured out how to fund a new building and construction started. Many staff members came to see it while it was being built, but I didn't, because at that time I hated the idea of a new place. I wanted to stay at my old familiar building until I retired, because I only had three years left. Why should I have to move to the new building? But

Madonna King wanted the Adoption Department to move into the new building, so I had to move. I only came here for the first time on the day we moved my boxes into my new office! I had never come before to see it while it was being built. Do you know, only a week later, I came to love it, because it looks so beautiful and there's so much sun. When we walk through the door, I feel like I've arrived at a rich home. And when our children grow up and come to the agency, they might have a "This was my home before" feeling. So I came to love it and I loved every single morning I arrived at my office. I do not take the elevator, I always take the stairs and I love each step. It's beautiful.

This agency goes in different directions, and I love all those changes. I love the many languages that are going on in this building, because of all the specialists. I used to be the only adoption staff member who was from a different country and spoke a different language besides broken English. But now we have so many; we have an international potluck lunch several times a year. That's wonderful. So the agency changed. It really changed. It became Children's Home Society & Family Services (CHSFS), with better and more valuable programs when we merged with the Family Services agency in St. Paul.

Our president also became very international, as Madonna King likes to travel on behalf of the different country programs and see the cultures. She is very good at developing new relationships. She is like an ambassador from our agency, because she goes to many places, some of them very poor, and she eats any food. That's amazing to me; even I cannot eat some of that food sometimes!

Dr. King was actually amazing to me from the very beginning, when we found out that a woman was going to take over as president of the agency. Before I even met her, I was worried and started to pray for her, that she would be a strong leader and a successful fund-raiser and a good person. I needn't have worried; she became a great boss, and one of the dearest persons to me. She provided lots of support to international adoption, and was always interested in the details of our programs. She let me be involved in some of her plans, and I thank her for that. She treated me in a very, very loving way. She has even invited me to serve as a member of the CHSFS Board of Directors, where I look forward to continuing my work on behalf of children in this new capacity. I am particularly honored, as I understand that I am the first staff person to be invited to serve on the Board.

Dr. King was my "big" boss, because she was the President. My main boss was Mr. David Pilgrim. I've known him since I came here in 1971. I think he was Volunteer Coordinator at that time, then he became a Social Worker, then Supervisor, then Director, and now he's a Vice President! He's been a long-time colleague, and my boss for a long time too. Mr. Pilgrim has always been wonderfully supportive of everything I've done, and what the Korean team was doing. And he was involved not only officially, but also personally, because he was always one to make sure I got help if I needed it, including in the other parts of my life that were not part of my work.

I've had many great colleagues throughout my years at Children's Home, so many that I better not try to name any more, or I might leave some out. I've also worked with a great number of kind, generous and wonderful adoptive parents, so many parents and so many colleagues that I came to feel that I'm rich because of all these people in my life. Without them, I would not feel that Minnesota is my home.

I will miss Children's Home and the work I did there, but I hope I can go on seeing the families and the children from time to time. Even as I write this, I'm having a lot of tears.

Those were some of the highlights of my professional career. I was very proud to represent CHSM and to be recognized for my work in Korean adoption. But I think my greatest accomplishments are hung on my office walls: photos of children and families for whom I helped find homes. What a blessing.

American Life

After my first trip to America through TCIP, my husband became more determined than ever to move our family there permanently. I never wanted to give up our life in Korea, and so we fought for the next four years until we sold our house and land and moved to Minnesota in 1975.

In 1980, we applied for citizenship. Applicants had to wait until their fifth year of residency to apply, but we were able to convince officials to let us file our applications six months early. My husband could not wait. He was only a few months away from realizing his lifelong dream since the Korean War. This was why he insisted on moving to America: he wanted to become a U.S. citizen and return to the only place he considered home, North Korea. Carefully, we collected all the required documents and filled in every line on our applications. I had done some traveling for work and had to keep a detailed log of where I had been and why. We studied for our tests and checked and double-checked every single form. My husband did not want to risk rejection. At one point, we had a scare. We had to be fingerprinted. My husband's went fine but when it was my turn, I blotted once then twice then three times. The official examined my hands and looked at me strangely. He asked, "Why don't you have any fingerprints?" The signature lines on my fingers that made up my print had been dulled from all my years of hard work: working with my hands, preparing food for work events, as well as for family and friends.

Finally, we became U.S. citizens in 1980 or 1981, and six months later, my husband returned home. All of his sacrifices, all of our family's, never were to be realized, though. My husband's parents had died before he got a chance to see them again.

That was the beginning of our American life.

Settling in

My son was very disappointed with our apartment on Eustis Street in St. Paul. To his five-year-old eyes, our new home looked like a box. "Mother, our house in Korea was much, much better than this," he said. He had never seen an apartment before. In Korea, there weren't many apartment complexes yet. Although Mr. Toogood had made sure we had a shower and provided us with dishes and pots and pans, we didn't have furniture. For meals, we sat on the floor because we didn't have a table; we slept in sleeping bags because we had no beds. There was a constant wing-wing-wing noise coming from within the wall (a bee had gotten trapped inside the wall). Although we told the landlord, it was a long while before it was taken care of and we didn't feel we should remind him, in case he thought we were complaining. Those were our first weeks in America. We arrived in mid-June, and I started work on July 1. Fortunately, I was able to walk to work but my husband still had to find a job.

Eventually we got settled and bought furniture and a car, but we needed to find a school for the children first. My former host mother from Highland Park helped us select a school. She insisted that we send our children to a private school, but we told her we could not afford the tuition. I don't know how she did it, but she got a private Catholic school to give my children the first-ever full scholarship. All we had to pay was bus fare. The school was in Mendota Heights and really was wonderful. But it was not easy to find a place to live on a bus route for the next three months. Finally we had to buy our first house, in the Highland Park neighborhood of St. Paul. We found that house with the help of my kind host mother, Mrs. Harris, who also found scholarships from the school and from the Jewish Community Center for my children.

Once that was taken care of, I needed to find the children some activities to fill up the rest of the summer before school started. Because I was working all day, I needed to send them to some sort of day camp. They ended up at Highland Park Jewish Community Center Summer Day Camp. Again, it was free because they offered my children full scholarships with the help of Mrs. Harris. I think they thought because we were immigrants, we were very poor. Every morning, my children walked a few blocks to the Como-Eustis bus stop and rode the bus to camp. Each afternoon, they came home the same way.

After a week, my son had blisters all over his tender feet. He had never walked so much before and he was miserable. He said he didn't want to go anymore, but I told him his sister went, I went to work, his father was looking for a job. If he stayed home, I told him, he would be all alone. He said that was fine. I told him to stay inside and warned him not to cry out loud in case someone heard him. You see, I had heard that it was illegal to leave a small child at home alone, but I had no choice and went to work at my office on Como. Soon after I arrived at work, I called home. "*Omma*, I'm scared," my son cried out. So I ran from Como Avenue back to the apartment on Snelling Avenue—three times in one day. My son kept crying because he was afraid of being home alone. At that time, I never thought I could stay home with him, even for one day. I've regretted that for a long time.

The next day, my son said he was going back to camp. He suffered the rest of that summer with blisters on his feet and taking swimming lessons, even though he hated the water (my children had never swam in Korea, but once we moved to America, my daughter was swimming like a fish in no time). The other problem my children faced at camp was a language barrier; they did not speak English yet. Fortunately, this camp attracted many children from other countries. In fact, my daughter ended up in the community newspaper because she befriended a girl from Russia, and even though they did not speak a common language, they became friends.

Shinhee

My daughter was twelve years old (Korean age) when we moved to America, about the same age I was when the Korean War broke out. My job as a social worker kept me very busy and I had to travel frequently. When I went on work trips, I usually made up a lot of food and froze it so Shinhee could take it out later and reheat it in a pan for her father. Funny thing, her father never knew about our arrangement. When I came back, he said, "Our daughter cooked! She cooks just like you do!" I smiled; she had done a good job.

Our house was like a hotel. Always, we seemed to have guests, either family or friends or visiting social workers I hosted. As a result, my daughter had to help me with the household duties because I still had work to do in the office during the days. I made her lists: clean the house; cook meals; prepare rooms for the guests; watch after her little brother. Like me, she had to help take care of her family at a young age. Many times she had to give up her own bedroom for guests and relocate to the basement. After about six months of this—moving up, then downstairs, and back up and down again, she made her room in the basement. I felt bad for her and wished she could have her room back, but she said she was happier downstairs rather than always moving room to room.

Growing up, Shinhee felt like Cinderella, and I was her wicked stepmother who made her cook and clean the house while I entertained guests. My son, too, said the same thing. They sometimes felt as if I were a stepmother because I made them work so hard. Years later, I think my daughter was thankful to learn how to cook at such a young age. Now she can cook anything. If she goes to a restaurant and tries a dish she likes, she can go home and make it exactly the same. She became an excellent cook. In fact, once my nephew from Korea came to stay with us for a while, and in his honor, Shinhee made a different food from a different country for an entire week. Everyone was excited trying something different in the beginning of the week, but by the end, my nephew asked if Shinhee would be leaving soon because he wanted regular Korean food. But like I said, she grew up to be a great cook, admired by her friends.

Shinhee struggled for her first six months in school. You see, back then the private schools did not offer special English classes for non-native speakers; everyone was thrown together and expected to keep up. Because my daughter had a hard time understanding her classmates and teachers, she spent the class periods drawing. She was very artistic and could draw well, so that was how she passed the time. Her classmates noticed her drawings and soon lined up at her desk after class, asking her to draw them something. She became rather popular, and although she wasn't able to communicate those first few months in English, she had found a way to communicate through her art. Six months later, she came home and said, "Ma! I can finally hear now."

I asked her, "You weren't able to hear all this time?" She said no, now she could understand: the English just one day hit her, and she understood. Just like that.

My first parent-teacher meeting was with Shinhee's history teacher. Because my children were attending a private Catholic school, many of their teachers were nuns. I asked the teacher if my daughter was doing well.

"She is not doing well in my class," the nun said.

"Really? Why not?" I said.

"Shinhee always has an odd, desperate-like look on her face," the nun explained. "Is your daughter okay? Why does she always look so confused and helpless all the time?"

Irritated, I asked the teacher, "Have you talked to my daughter's other teachers? What have they said?"

"All her other teachers say she's doing fine," the nun said. "Only in my class is she doing badly."

I explained to this teacher that we had recently moved to America from Korea and my daughter was learning English for the first time. The nun said she had no idea; nobody mentioned that to her, not even the other teachers. Continuing, I told the nun that my daughter had told me about her history class and the fact that she had a very hard time understanding her teacher because the teacher spoke too fast. The teacher apologized, and I hoped she would understand and maybe slow down her speech. When I left that day, I understood how hard this move was on my children.

My children continued to attend that school for the next two to three years, but then the school asked if we could pay a small amount of tuition. My husband refused and said that it was time to move them to public school. Both my children loved their school, and they begged to stay at the same school, but instead we enrolled them in the Highland Park public schools. My daughter was entering junior high and my son was in grade school.

They hated it.

"Ma, what's welfare?" Shinhee asked me one day after school. By this time, she and my son had learned English and had no problems understanding their classes and their friends at school.

"Why?" I asked.

"Just tell me," she said.

I explained it to her and suddenly she looked very mad.

"I'm packing our bags!" she announced.

Something had happened. She told me that some girls at school had asked her where she was from, and she explained that she was from Korea. They asked her why her family didn't have an American-sounding last name. Confused, Shinhee said because they are Korean. One of the girls said, "Oh, you're not adopted?" Shinhee told them no, she was not adopted. The girls giggled and said that they thought all Korean children were adopted, so if Shinhee wasn't then it meant that hers was a refugee family that lived on welfare. They laughed again. Not understanding "welfare," my daughter had nothing to say until she came home and I explained to her what the girls meant. The next day she went back to school and said to the girls: "My mother had a job the first day we arrived here, and my father got a job the first day, so what do you mean we live on welfare?" The girls finally apologized.

I wanted my daughter to become a medical doctor because I knew that doctors made a lot of money and they were well-respected. When she went to college, I suggested that Shinhee enroll in physics, chemistry and biology, but she did not do well in them. She said: "Ma, I am going to flunk." I told her to change her schedule, so she dropped some classes. "You are strong in mathematics," I told her. "You can be a CPA." Her second year she switched to math and accounting classes, but had to drop them too. I suggested that she take another major, whatever she liked. By her third year she had taken child psychology and did really well. Even though she had switched her classes and majors so many times because of her mom's bad advice, I was amazed she was able to still graduate on time. Her undergraduate degree was in child psychology.

When it was time to apply for graduate schools, she told me she wanted to stay with psychology.

I moaned. "I am a social worker and yet I gave birth to a daughter who is good in math so I thought she might have a brighter future. Now she wants to get her Master's in Child Psychology?"

I explained to her that if she did her Master's in psychology she would not be able to find a practical job after graduation, and so she must go into social work, if that was the field she was interested in. With a social work degree, I knew that there would always be jobs out there for her. So she enrolled at the University of Minnesota with a major in social work, but she became very depressed; this was not where she wanted to go. One of her professors pulled her aside and told her about the University of Chicago's program.

Shinhee carefully prepared all the financial aid applications in detail, including loans and scholarships. For the first time, she asked if we could help her for a small part of the cost. (She paid her own way all the way through her undergraduate degree.) We were very glad that she asked for some help, because she had not done so before.

Top: *1964 ~ International Social Services (ISS) with a foster mother, three foster kids who were going to the U.S. and other staff members and escorts.*

Above: *Mrs. Han with daughter Shinhee at age six. Doll from Hong Kong brought by husband. Drew pictures and was a good artist.*

Right: *Mrs. Han with Shinhee at age 2¹/₂*

Top: *1976 ~ Mrs. Han with Jeff Mondloh for CHSM post-adoption talk.*

Bottom: *1978 ~ Mrs. Han [front row, left] visted Korea. Whole family gathered.*

Top: *Early 1980s with ECWS social workers who came to CHSM for training.*

Bottom: *1981 ~ Mrs. Han with CHSM staff to celebrate her becoming a U.S. citizen*

Top: *Mrs. Han with Roger Toogood*

Top: *1995 ~*
Last family photo,
one month before
Mr. Han died.

Opposite Page

Top: *passport photos*
for immigration

Bottom: *family*
photo in 1978

Above: *1994 ~ Family gathering, a few months before Mr. Han died.*

Top: 2000 ~ *Celebrating Mother's 80th birthday in South Korea with all family members. [Han, back row, 5th from left; mother seated 2nd from left]*

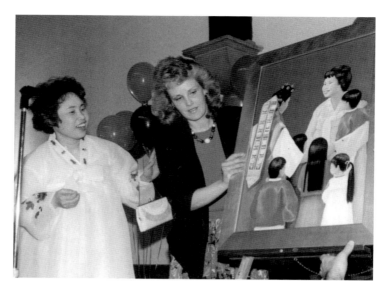

Top: *1989 ~ May 11, Governor's proclamation of Mrs. Han Day, with Mary Janssen, an adoptive parent.*
Bottom: *1991 ~ Mrs. Han [center] received award from Child Welfare League of America*

Top: *1990 ~ Hand in Hand Forever, quilt*
made for Korean Benefit Dinner fundraiser

Top: *1980 ~*
Mrs. Han with
adopted children

Above: *1980 ~*
Mrs. Han with
Korean guests visiting
an American home.

Left: *1979 ~*
Mrs. Han [right] in a
play at church during
Christmas time.

Top: *Church choir, member for 14 years. [Han second row, 2nd from right; Mr. Han top row, 2nd from left]*

Above: *1980 ~ Mrs. Han [second from left], ECWS social workers at Korean Benefit Dinner.*

Bottom: *1985 ~ Mrs. Han with Mary Fonken, an adoptive parent.*

Top: *1998 ~ Son's wedding with both mothers.*

Bottom: *2001 ~ Mrs. Han [left] at Shinhee's graduation; Ph.D in social work at New York University, with 2nd sister.*

Top: *1997 ~ In North Korea with husband's 2nd sister and her son.*

Bottom: *1997 ~ In North Korea with village leader of sister-in-law. In front of picture of North Korean leader Kim Il Sung.*

Left and Bottom: 2003 ~
At 25th Anniversary of
Korean Benefit event with
Madonna King and guests.

Below: 2003 ~
Celebrating Mrs. Han's
retirement at CHSFS [from
left to right] with Roger
Toogood, Madonna King,
Ron Reed, President
Emeritus Family Services,
Inc., and David Pilgrim

Top: *December 2003 ~ At retirement party held at ECWS, Korea. Mrs. Han seated next to Dr. Kim and Dr. Kim.*

Right: *Lighting the celebration cake with both Dr. Kims and Madonna King.*

Below: *Mrs. Han with Dr. Kim's daughter, David Pilgrim and Madonna King.*

2002 ~ with son's children, Alex and Aaron.

When I found that the school was located in downtown Chicago, I became very scared. I went to orientation with her and saw that many other parents had the same concerns as I did. The school explained that they did their best to protect students and make the campus safe; they had student escort services and good security in student housing. Students in New York were mugged sometimes, but not Chicago students, the school said. I felt better.

While she worked toward her Master's degree, Shinhee did various volunteer jobs, some translating and part-time work at an adoption agency in Chicago. I was very proud of her hard work. My husband and I attended her graduation and helped her move into an apartment. We drove two cars to Chicago because we were giving Shinhee one of them, so I followed my husband through downtown Chicago. Now, my husband believed he was the best driver in the whole world but as I followed him into the busy downtown streets I wondered: if he's such a good driver, why does he change lanes so often? What is he doing? I was so nervous and had to follow him so closely, jumping lane to lane, making sure that I didn't lose him. Finally, when we arrived at the school he got out of the car and said to me: "You are a good follower." I thought: I had no choice or I would've been lost. Anyway, we delivered the old car to Shinhee so she could use it for work. We were very proud of our daughter. She took out loans for most of her schooling and paid it all back herself; she was very good with her money management, and still is.

After completing her Master's, my daughter was hired as a counselor at the University of Chicago. For many years she used our old car to drive home to visit us often, but then she moved to New York to work at Columbia University and complete her Ph.D. at NYU, and she wasn't able to visit as frequently. I also went to New York to attend that graduation. At first, Shinhee told me not to come. "I'm not even going," she said. "It's not that big of a deal." I told her that this was her final graduation and that I wanted to come and wanted her to attend the ceremony. When I got there, though, I had gotten sick, and could only attend the ceremony. She had planned a lot of activities for us to do but I had to stay inside on the couch and rest. While I was resting, I read her entire thesis over the next three days. I think she really appreciated that.

Shin Up

Not long after we had settled into our new life in America, the doorbell rang. I opened it and found about seven or eight little boys on my doorstep. "Can we play with Mike?" they said.

"Mike?" I repeated. "We don't have a Mike here. Maybe you have the wrong house."

"No, we have the right house," they said. "You have a Mike. It's your son."

I yelled for Shin Up. "Are you Mike?" I asked him.

My son said yes and ran out the door to play with his friends before I could question him further. At dinner time, I asked him about his name change. He explained that the first time he went out to play, the neighborhood boys had asked him what his name was. He said, "Shin Up Han." They asked him again: what is your first name? My son knew that Americans didn't understand Korean names, so he said the first American name that came to his head: "My name is Mike," he told his new friends. You see, my former host mother had suggested that we give our children American names once they started school; that way, they would fit in better and others would be able to pronounce their names easily. My husband and I had talked about different American names but had trouble finding ones we liked. For our daughter, we thought of Jeannie because it was close to her Korean name, Shinhee, but she didn't like it because it made her think of "genie" as in the genie in the lamp. We tried Mary, but that was too funny to our ears. Shinhee didn't like that name at all, so she chose to keep her Korean name. Besides, her name had simple and familiar sounds to American ears so it was not too difficult to pronounce.

As for our son: my husband liked "David" or "Mike." In fact, he wanted to use David for himself, and Mike for our son, but I didn't agree. We talked about it for some time, but never quite finished the conversation. I think Shin Up heard us talking, and said that he wanted to use Mike as his first name, and that's why he quickly said "Mike" when the boys asked his first name. We let him keep the name and registered him as Mike Shin Up Han when he started school.

The first couple of months of school were difficult for my son. He had learned English quickly but it took longer for him to fit in with the school kids, many of whom yelled "chink!" at him and his sister as they walked to the school bus stop each morning. Even more difficult for my son was balancing his Korean upbringing with his new American life.

I received a call from the school principal because of my son. She called me during the day at work and she said my son had told his teacher to "shut up." I apologized and waited for my son to come home from school to talk to him. Mike came home that day with swollen, red eyes; I saw that he had been crying. Once my son starts crying, he cries forever. So I asked him what had happened at school. At first he said "nothing," but I kept talking and finally he explained that during the games they played at recess he and another boy were fighting over a ball. Both of them declared it, "mine!" The teacher saw what was going on and talked to both boys, but Mike grabbed the ball again and started to cry. He said it was his ball. His teacher realized that he hadn't understood her—not just the words but also the cultural rules. So the teacher had Mike stay longer after the bell rang that signaled recess was over. She sat out on the steps with him and tried to explain the rules to him. Mike stood up suddenly and, red-faced, he shouted, "Shut up!" His teacher was very embarrassed and angry with his outburst, so she reported it to the principal as bad behavior.

My son explained to me that his teacher was talking and talking and talking, and he wanted to hurry back to class because this was milk-and-cookies time, and he didn't want to miss his afternoon snack. Besides, he told me, he didn't understand her any better. My son was only five years old; he just wanted his snack. Because his English still was limited and he was so young, he didn't know how to explain himself and the only words he knew that could tell the teacher to stop talking were "shut up," which he had learned from another child. I called the principal the next day and explained, also pointing out that we didn't use the word "shut up" in our house so it was a word my son had learned at school. The principal apologized for the mix-up, but that wasn't the last of the cultural misunderstandings.

Mike came home from school crying one day. I asked him what was wrong. He said his sister was mad at him because he had called her "sister" in the school hallway, in front of everyone. They were attending the private Catholic school then, so all their teachers were nuns and were referred to as "sisters." When Mike shouted out to Shinhee in the hallway, "sister," one of the nuns turned around and said, "Yes, Mike?" Mike explained that he meant his sister, not the teacher, Sister.

You see, *Nuna* was the Korean word for older sister, and that was what my son had always called his sister; in Korea, it was not proper to call each other by first names. The polite way to address one another was to call each other by title and relationship. Mike had directly translated the Korean word for sister into the English and ended up embarrassing Shinhee. Confused, Mike thought maybe his sister wanted to be called by her first name, like an American. The next day at school he called out, "Shinhee!" His sister didn't reply; inside, the Korean in her was insulted to be called by her first name. You see, Mike was much younger than my daughter, and in Korea, it was rude to call one's elder by her first name. Poor Mike. He came home that night and at dinner he said, "What should I call you?" My daughter thought about it; my husband thought about it; I thought about it. Finally, we agreed on *"Nuna."* That was what Mike called her at home, that was what she was used to in Korea, so we decided that would be fine to use in school. Nobody would understand, anyway. Do you know what happened? Pretty soon all her classmates and even her teachers began calling her *Nuna*. They heard her brother use the name and mistook it as her given name. We thought that was very funny. In Korea, it was a word that showed respect to an older sibling; in America, my daughter's teachers—older adults—were calling her by a respectful title.

Mike had turned ten when my husband and I were preparing our citizenship papers. For several nights, we had paperwork to do and Mike wondered why we had "homework."

"Son, this is not homework," I explained. "We are applying for citizenship. We are going to become American citizens."

Mike's face lit up. "Yeah!" he said. "Now the school kids won't tease me anymore."

This was a surprise to me. He hadn't said anything about anyone teasing him. My husband became very upset at hearing this and asked Mike what the kids called him.

"Well, of course they call me 'chink,'" Mike said. "You know they also call me slanty-eyes and dirty knees."

"So you think that if we become American citizens they won't tease you anymore?" I asked.

"Right," Mike said. "I will become just like them."

About a year after we had become citizens, I remembered this story and checked back in with my son. "So, now that you are a citizen, does anyone tease you?"

"Are you kidding?" Mike said. "I'm the same. I look the same. Nothing changed."

I realized then that my son had misunderstood. He thought that becoming an American also meant that he would become white. The teasing had not stopped and so my husband asked Mike what he did about it. "Do you just listen?" my husband asked. He wanted to know if Mike knew how to stand up for himself.

"No, I call them 'honky' back," Mike reported. Somehow, from somewhere, my son had learned that word, and he used it to fight back.

After we moved our children into public school, they came home with all kinds of strange ideas. One night, Mike came home and cried, "If you and dad die, will I be adopted again?" My daughter promised him that she would take care of him if that happened, but my son knew that she could not raise him. She was only a child. I didn't understand why this was a concern all of a sudden and pried further. Turns out, there were some kids at school who were in foster care. He had heard stories about foster care kids being moved from family to family because no one wanted them. Up until then, he had only heard positive stories about adoption. Oh, I was frustrated with those kids for making my son worry. I assured him that he would not have to live in a foster family or be adopted again, because my two younger brothers (his uncles) would raise him with his sister if anything happened to us. That seemed to calm him down.

Junior high

One night, Mike was misbehaving and I scolded him so badly he refused to come to dinner and eat. I was angry with him, so I let him sulk and we ate dinner without him. After dinner, I went upstairs to check on him and found that he was crying. He was in eighth grade then, and I thought it was silly for a boy his age to cry just because I scolded him. I thought he was acting like a child. My daughter intervened and said she would talk to him. Mike told his sister what had happened at school that day, and why he was so sensitive when I scolded him; he was still feeling badly and getting yelled at by his mother was more than he could handle. After Shinhee talked to Mike she came out and told me what had happened, even though Mike had made her promise not to tell me. "If you tell Mom this story, you are no longer my sister," he warned.

Mike was the teacher's pet at school, Shinhee said, and also an excellent student with very good grades. And being Korean was part of it. Because of those things, the other students were always making fun of him. That particular day, some of the boys were throwing their books while the teacher had stepped out of the room. These were heavy books, and Mike shouted at them to stop it. One of the boys wrestled

Mike to the floor and began choking my son. "I thought I was going to die," he told his sister. "I couldn't breathe.

"So I was upset when I came home and then Mom started in on me and that was more than I could take. That just made me even sadder."

Oh, after I heard that story, I cried, too. I couldn't say anything to Mike because Shinhee wasn't supposed to tell me, so inside I felt awful. Mostly, I felt bad not because of what happened to my son but because all along this was going on, he was being teased in school for being the teacher's pet and being Korean, and I had no idea, even though I was his mother. There I was, a social worker who gave advice and speeches to adoptive parents about the prejudices their adopted Korean children might face, and yet I couldn't even care for my own son.

A few days later I approached Mike and confessed that I knew what had happened, making sure that he didn't blame his sister for tattling. I told him that I was going to do something about it because it wasn't right for me to sit back and do nothing. Mike told me not to say anything. "Mother, if you tell anyone at my school, I will stop going!" he threatened. He was serious. "This is my problem," Mike continued. "I will handle it; don't ever try to help." What could I do? For a long time after that, I checked his face every day after school, afraid that he might have been beat up again. I worried and worried for him each day, until he entered high school.

You know, when it comes to your own child, it is hard to take your own advice. I was so hurt when I heard about what was happening to Mike. Worse, all I could do was worry; I could not help. When I went to his junior high for conferences later, I found out that his math teacher was

Japanese. I asked Mike about it later, wondering why he hadn't mentioned this, and my son said he never thought about it. To Mike, he was just his math teacher. I was glad, though, to talk to the teacher and realize that this man tried to help his minority students the best he could. My son got a lot of support from this teacher in ways my son didn't always recognize or understand at that age.

My son survived his junior high years and he did make some lifetime friends. In fact, he still gets together with many of them, as well as high school pals. For that, I am glad.

Mike was the best son—until he turned seventeen. Up until then he was a model student and always obeyed his parents. I couldn't have asked for a better son. My daughter back then was very strong-willed and had a mind of her own. I didn't know my son was the same until he became seventeen.

During my son's turbulent years, I learned a lesson. When my son was younger, I was helping adoptive parents who were struggling with their teenaged adopted children. When they told me their troubles, I thought how I had a son who was adopted, and he was no trouble at all. So in my mind, I blamed the parents; they were the problem, not their children. My attitude changed when my son became a teenager. All of a sudden, I understood what those parents had been telling me. I cried for the parents and cried for the children. I came to understand both sides of the story. Eventually, I learned to change my own attitude and became a better social worker for that experience. I understood that when problems arise, the parents must change their own attitudes and try to effect change in that way; they cannot expect their child to change. Parents need patience; they need to adjust their expectations. Love is different in every family. After that, whenever adoptive parents told me about their children's problems with tears in their eyes, I cried together with them many times. Once I understood that, I changed myself rather than thinking my son had to change, and in the end, I became a better Christian.

American life

Our first house in America was in Highland Park, and we lived there until about 1980. We might have lived there longer if my husband had not sold our home to his friend. You see, I had gone to Korea for some agency business and when I came back my husband had sealed the deal with his friend. The friend had moved to America from Korea (probably at my husband's urging) and needed a place to live. He could not afford to pay full price for a house and, not having a credit history in America, he was unable to secure a bank loan, so my husband offered him our house. They agreed that the friend would make payments to my husband, just as he would the bank. When I returned from my trip, my husband announced that we were moving.

My husband had found two houses out of fifty that he and his friend had looked at while I was gone; they narrowed it down to two for me to choose from. One was in Mounds View, which was a brand new house not even finished being built, and one in Fridley. The Mounds View home was on a hilly plot, and I preferred a flat one for the children to play in, so we ended up moving to Fridley. It took me five years to like that house. For those five years, I blamed him for making that agreement without asking me. We fought a lot for a while. Funny thing, I still live in that house: twenty-three years. I still think our Highland Park house was better built, but I have come to love Fridley.

When we were looking at houses in Highland Park, I remember some of the neighborhood people watching us carefully and as soon as we moved in, everyone heard. We were the first Korean family to move into the area, and I often wondered if people thought their property values would decline because of the "Orientals." But we soon found out how much we all had in common. Shortly after we moved in, one of the neighbor ladies came by to introduce herself. We talked a while and she asked me if my husband was a medical doctor. I told her no, he was not. Does he teach at the University of Minnesota, she asked? No, he just works at a company. She was surprised, and even more so when she found out that I worked full-time as a social worker. However, she was not the one to remain taken aback; my surprise was the discovery that she was an adoptive parent who had adopted a son and a daughter from the agency I worked for. Soon, word got out around the neighborhood that I was a social worker at CHSM, and I found out that several families in the area were adoptive families themselves, either from CHSM or Catholic Charities or Lutheran Social Services. All of the neighborhood adoptees were Caucasian back then, except for one baby who was from Vietnam.

A week before we moved to Fridley, I invited a few neighbor ladies over for lunch. As I was chopping vegetables, I felt a sudden sharp pain in my elbow, and ended up rolling around on the floor crying out in pain. Luckily, some of my friends happened to stop by, and they found me crying. They took me to the hospital and had some X-rays done. We discovered that the cartilage that served as cushioning between my bones had worn out from all the cooking I had been doing. The doctor was surprised to hear that a social worker had developed such a problem. I explained that when I started at CHSM, I often cooked Korean food for as many as three hundred guests, like at the Korean Benefit Dinners. I cooked for family, friends and large and small CHSM events. You see, Korean food requires a lot of preparation; you have to chop everything up. Within five years of moving to America and working at CHSM, I had trouble moving my arm for a while. By the time we moved into our Fridley home, my arms were immobile, so my friends had to help for the first month. My hand and arm healed, only to have the same thing happen, five years later, to my left side.

Hosting Korean guests

Back then, CHSM didn't have much of a budget to entertain all the visitors from Korea. It was my idea to bring Korean social workers, orphanage directors and others to America to see CHSM's work in international adoptions. At that time, Koreans were very negative about international adoptions and I believed that if they saw how it worked on the American side, they would come to understand it better and then help us promote the positives of adoption in Korea. I had told the director, Mr. Toogood, not to worry; I put all the visitors up in my house and provided all their meals—on top of my full-time work at the agency. I kept that up for the next fifteen years, and CHSM never had to pay any of the expense. Another reason for my having to cook was that there were no Korean restaurants yet. No matter how many people came, they stayed at our house. At least seventy people came through my house in any given year. My neighbors got curious. "What are you doing?" they asked. "Are you running a guest house? We always see people going in and out, carrying lots of luggage." I explained that we were trying to expose Koreans to adoption in America because back then, Koreans thought adoption was bad; they believed Americans were adopting Korean children in order to turn them into servants or use them as organ donors. CHSM wanted to show them the reality of adoption. If I didn't help host our Korean guests, we wouldn't have been able to continue to invite Korean people who had a connection to international adoption. These included government officials, media people, orphanage directors, adoption agency social workers, and so on.

One time, we were hosting five ladies who represented five different provincial government child welfare departments from Korea. As usual, I made a bunch of Korean food. My husband was in charge of drinks and always offered our guests the liquor of their choice. Most guests drank beer, but these ladies drank the real liquor. Wah, they could drink! One of the ladies was taking a shower when my husband was serving drinks, so she came down to dinner late. My husband offered her a drink that looked like a Coke. Without a pause, she drank the whole glass in one swallow; I think she was still hot from the shower and needed something to quench her thirst. Five minutes later, she passed out. We had to drag her into her room, and she slept through the night. Apparently, my husband had added a little alcohol to that Coke, and she had never had any alcohol in her life, and never asked if there was anything in the Coke before she took it. She later said that she woke up during the night, very very hungry. That became one of our funnier stories over the years.

We didn't get regular sleep in those days. I remember when we received a call from a famous designer in Korea at two o'clock in the morning.

"Hello, my name is Andre Kim," the stranger said. "Is this Mrs. Han?"

"Yes, this is," I said.

"One of my customers told me about you and gave me your telephone number," Mr. Kim continued. "I will be visiting your city soon. I have friends all over the world, but none in Minneapolis, so I was wondering if you would be my guide. I will be staying two nights and three days."

"Okay," I said.

After I got off the phone, my husband asked, "What dumb person is calling at such an hour?" I was too tired to talk about it and told him I'd explain it to him the next day. When I finally told my husband who the strange caller was, he couldn't believe it. "What?" he exclaimed. "How do you know such a famous Korean designer?" I explained that someone had given Mr. Kim my name and number. Before his visit, Mr. Kim called a few more times, and always around one or two o'clock in the morning. I don't think he realized the time difference. Finally he arrived, excited to see our famous Mall of America. Unfortunately, he came in the middle of winter—and right in the midst of a major snowstorm. He didn't seem to mind, though. Because I didn't know my way around the Mall very well, I asked a friend and her son to help show Mr. Kim around. They were excited to meet a famous Korean designer. We all had a great time with Mr. Kim. I cooked dinner for all of us one night. On the next evening, he invited all of us to the Shilla Restaurant. Instead of having each person order one item, he ordered many, many dishes for everyone to share, just like I would have done for guests at home. He insisted that it was my turn to enjoy someone else's cooking. Oh, he was a wonderful guest. He later mailed me one of his designer jackets!

Another fun party was when the people from KBS (Korean Broadcasting System), the number one station in Seoul, came to visit. They were making a special program about adoption and did some filming here. The agency provided money for hotels and meals, but this group didn't want to eat in restaurants or stay in a nice hotel. They wanted to stay at our house. I think there were eight or nine of them. They really liked to have a good time. One night, they were drunk and dancing and singing and shouting loudly. I worried about our neighbor making a complaint to the police. My husband, however, thought the group was really fun. He couldn't bear to just sit and watch, and he didn't want to worry about the neighbor, so he phoned our neighbor and invited him over. That night, all of us sat up with those KBS people and laughed and laughed until three in the morning. Oh, what a fun party!

Once, a very important visitor came from Korea, the top family welfare bureau chief. He was only going to be in Minnesota for two evenings, so I planned to invite him to dinner in my home for the first night, then on the second night my Executive Director and I and other CHSM people would take him to a fine restaurant. When he came to my home the first night, he had such a great time with my husband and enjoyed himself so much that he asked to come to my home again the second night, instead of going to a restaurant. So that's what we did, and we all had a wonderful time.

Other times weren't so fun. One time a government official came to visit. We got such a bad snowstorm during his visit that we couldn't leave the house. For three nights and four days we were stuck in the house. I felt so bad. We couldn't take him sightseeing or even go buy groceries; we had to eat what was in the refrigerator. But he was in good cheer. "This will be the story of my lifetime," he said. "I'll tell this to all my family and friends for a long time." Why? Because he had never seen so much snow. He was amazed, and we were thankful for having such an easy-going guest.

Those exchanges were great successes. The Korean social workers and directors got to see how adoption worked here in the States and went back to Korea to tell people that intercountry adoption was a very good thing. Our exchange program helped eliminate all the myths about adoption in Korea.

After fifteen years of hosting all of the CHSM Korean visitors, the agency finally was able to put up our guests in hotel rooms. However, I still made a lot of the food because no one else knew how to prepare Korean food. Today, there are Korean restaurants and the agency is able to pay for everything for our guests.

During all those years of entertaining, I felt bad for my daughter. She always had to sleep in the basement so guests could sleep in her bed. She also was the one who helped with all the cooking because I was working full-time and didn't get home until five or six o'clock at night. She was twelve years old. Later, she told me she believed she was a stepchild because only a stepchild would have to give up her bedroom and constantly cook for guests. One good thing did come of it. She became an excellent cook. In fact, she's much better than I am.

My husband was a great help during those years, too. He didn't always like having guests, or all the time and money I put into my job. He joked once that all the money I made in my job I ended up giving away by hosting Korean guests, and buying gifts whenever I went to Korea. But he was a great host, taking care of the guests' needs. Still, he sometimes felt neglected. He used to tell me that I wasn't a very good wife because I was always late, and I worked days and nights and weekends. At the same time he understood why I did what I did. "I really admire you because you are working for children," he said. "One human being is so important, and you are taking care of many, many souls. That's amazing." I guess that's why he was always willing to help with the guests. Even though they weren't his friends, he welcomed them as if they were. My husband was a great support. Without him, I don't think I could have done what I did. When I received the proclamation from the Governor years later, he was the happiest and proudest husband. He told everyone about it. In his own way, he was proud of me. He wasn't particularly proud of me as a wife or mother, but he was proud of my life's work. That was fair. I wasn't a very good wife or mother then. I was so busy with my work. My entire family made sacrifices so that I could maintain my dedication to my work. During that time, I didn't appreciate my husband enough. After his death, I finally understood what a great man he was. He wasn't an average husband. Few husbands would have supported my work like he did. He encouraged me to work for life, not for wealth, even though he joked that if I had worked that hard for money, we would've been millionaires. But my husband was right; my work has given me a wonderful life.

My
Husband

*I*n October, 1994, I had to go to Korea again for agency business. My flight was Monday morning, but I couldn't find my passport that morning. Then I remembered that I had put it in our safety deposit box at the bank for safekeeping; there was no way I could get it in time and make my flight. My husband said not to worry, and decided to turn my absent-minded mistake into a positive thing: he decided to go with me. Because I had to make new arrangements for myself, he decided to go last-minute and attend his nephew's wedding in November. We pushed my trip back two weeks. I left with a CHSM co-worker; my husband came a week later.

About six months before that trip my husband had complained about a lack of energy. He didn't appear to be sick; he was just always tired. He kept going to the doctor for the next five months, but the doctor didn't find anything wrong with my husband; he told my husband that he was fine. The tiredness persisted however, and finally, I told my husband: you are not fine. Something is very wrong. He went in for another check-up and tests before catching his flight to Korea. I met him at the airport with his cousin in Seoul. As he walked toward us, I saw that he had a strange look in his eyes; he had the look of someone who was just going through the motions of life but inside he had already died. He didn't look tired; he looked as if he had given up. His cousin asked, "Why do you look so terrible?" Afraid, I didn't say anything but watched my husband closely. He didn't eat much on that trip, but he attended the wedding and did all the things we planned to do while in Korea.

On the way back, we escorted two babies who were going to be adopted, one for me and one for him. They cried for most of the flight, but my husband wasn't able to help me with my crying baby as he was too tired out by his baby. Two days after we arrived home, we got a call from the doctor. My husband had liver cancer and the doctor estimated that he had two months left to live. I was so angry with the doctor, who seemed to deliver the news so callously. "You're going to die in two months," he told my husband. This was the same doctor who had just told him he was fine, the same one who had been telling my husband for the past six months that my husband was just fine. At the news, all of the strength drained out of me and I collapsed to the floor. My husband said nothing. I cried and cried, and from that day until my husband died, I didn't have the strength to say a real prayer. All I could do was cry out: "Oh God, Oh God"—and nothing more.

We went back to the doctor and he apologized. The tests he did right before my husband left for Korea were the ones that finally yielded some results. Unfortunately, he said, those results had come too late. My husband's liver cancer was in its final stages; there was no treatment to be done. All we could do was to go home and make his final days as comfortable as possible. Still I was angry. My husband had had two surgeries on his stomach after we first moved to America, so his doctor thought that condition might have come back. He only checked for possible stomach problems. No blood tests were done until it was too late. I thought: a blood test is basic; it's like A-B-C. Many men have liver problems, especially Asian men, I thought. Moreover, I was mad that we didn't know about my husband's cancer before he traveled overseas; I thought that shortened his life. My husband saw his trip as a good thing; he got to say a final goodbye to his family in Korea.

The next two months were busy. My husband insisted that he couldn't just tell people over the phone or over dinner that he was going to die in two months. Instead, he had an unusual idea. My husband was so funny that way. So we called up our best friends, two other couples, and we made plans to go to Las Vegas. My husband was the leader of our group, so they all agreed. We had done many trips before, like the time we got a big group of us to drive to Chicago in a line of twelve cars. Those were such fun times; we never did anything like that after my husband died.

At first, one of our friends said she couldn't make it, so I called her back and told her that if she didn't go, she would regret it for the rest of her life. She didn't understand but she heard the seriousness in my voice and agreed to adjust her plans so that she could go. We met the two couples at the airport, and I saw that one of his friends had brought a lawn chair. When I asked him why, he said he brought it for my husband. "Mr. Han looks so weak these days," he joked. "Why do you look so weak and tired? You are younger than me." My husband only smiled at the joke. Our friend did not know.

In Las Vegas, we had dinner together and that's when my husband told our friends. They didn't believe him at first. "I am telling the truth," my husband said. "I just found out a few days ago. I wanted us all to take this trip so we have this last memory forever."

Shinhee came and met us in Las Vegas. We got tickets to a show, but my husband wasn't feeling well enough that evening to go. He insisted that the rest of us go and simply let him rest. The next day, he gave me money and told me to go play the slot machines with Shinhee. After two days, leaving our friends and Shinhee in Las Vegas, I took him back to Minnesota and had him admitted to the hospital, as the internal bleeding had started.

As soon as the bleeding stopped, they sent him home. I think we went back once more due to internal bleeding, but beyond stopping the bleeding the hospital could do little else. I was very mad about that. I thought my husband needed around-the-clock medical care. How could they kick him out when he was so obviously sick? But while he was in the hospital for those short stays, over a hundred people came to visit him. He really didn't get much rest. Part of that was his fault; he refused to say no to anyone. He also insisted on greeting everyone while sitting up in a chair, not from his bed. Even one minute before he fell into a coma, he was sitting in a chair. He was a very polite person.

His room was filled with flowers. The nurses and doctors said they had never seen a patient receive so many flowers and wondered who he was. My husband loved those bouquets. He said, "I never knew flowers could be so beautiful. Now I see how they give their short lives to make us human beings happy."

My husband joked that he was going to go first and be the doorman for me in heaven. His spirits remained so much higher than mine. I loved that he still could joke and make me laugh.

A well-known Korean doctor who specialized in cancer treatments came to visit my husband after his first hospitalization. He told my husband he wished he had heard of my husband's condition earlier. "I could have helped you the most," the doctor said. "Now, I can't do a thing. Why didn't you think to call me?" My husband just smiled and joked with the doctor, thanking him for buying so many tickets from my husband's travel business over the years. The doctor was amazed by my husband's good humor. "I not only respect you, I worship you," the doctor told my husband. "I see many people who are dying in my profession, but I never met anyone who was as grateful and graceful and happy as you." That made my husband so happy, to be paid such a high compliment from such a highly respected man.

After my husband's second hospitalization, the doctor said it wasn't necessary to bring my husband back any longer. I had learned how to administer the dialysis shots so he could rest at home. In those final few weeks, he was so tired and weak he couldn't do much of anything. Around that time, a social work professor I knew from Korea who had come to Minnesota from New York (where she went for her doctorate degree) helped me around the house for about a week. She cleaned and cooked and helped entertain all the guests who stopped by to wish my husband well. I couldn't have done it without her; I was so busy caring for my husband, administering his shots and tending to his every need. All this time, I thought I had no choice; I didn't know that I could have had a nurse take care of all that. When I caught a cold, I made sure to wear a mask so my husband wouldn't catch pneumonia. Those days I cried all the time, so much so that my tears often blinded me and made it hard for me to administer his shot.

My daughter came near the end and planned to stay for as long as was necessary, but I told her she had to go back to work. She could not sit around the house and simply wait, so she reluctantly returned to New York. But she made sure she called every day, sometimes twice a day.

In his last few days, my husband asked when Shinhee would return home. That was Wednesday. I told him she could come back now if he wanted, but she was not due until Saturday. He said that was fine; she didn't need to change her plans. By Thursday, he stopped eating. Then he said there were too many people in his room. That's when I knew he had started to hallucinate. All our guests stayed downstairs. When I asked him who was in the room, he said he saw many old Korean men in white coats. He also said I think I am going to die soon. Twice, he saw those Korean men in white coats. At night he couldn't sleep, and three days before his last, he had almost completely lost his voice.

That Thursday, the pastor from the Presbyterian church stopped by with a jar of pumpkin soup. My husband couldn't even swallow then, but he took a spoonful to be polite. My husband and the pastor spoke while I went to the kitchen to prepare tea. Up until then, my husband had only said to me: you work very hard; thank you. I had no idea how he really felt until that pastor told my close friend, Mrs. Lee, what my husband had said while I was getting the tea. She was one of his church members, and she told me the story a month after the funeral. My husband had said: "Pastor, I never realized that my wife was such a great person. Now that I understand that, I am proud to say that she is a good person with big visions and a bigger heart." Oh, that made me so happy to know that my husband gave me such a big compliment to someone else.

On Friday, my husband asked for our daughter every hour. "Is she coming?" he said. I said: she will be here tomorrow. He seemed very antsy and anxious. I think he knew he was dying. There was no pain, just anxiety. He told me he didn't know what to do with himself; he felt so sick yet he felt like he couldn't keep still. Finally, Saturday morning came and our daughter arrived. My husband was sleeping but woke when she came into the room.

"You came!" he said. "I'm so happy you came. I'm so glad to see you."

At this point, his tummy had become bloated and his legs swollen. I told him he needed to walk a bit. Shinhee helped him as he took a few steps. I prepared him a bath, as he hadn't had one in days, but the bath was upstairs from his room so the professor, my daughter and I helped him to the bathroom. I helped him into the tub myself, and finally, he relaxed. "You are a very lucky person," I said as I bathed him. "Many people were killed during the Korean War, and you were a war orphan, only fourteen years old then but you have survived all this time." He agreed. As I washed and dried him he said, "I am a very lucky man. I can die in a happy environment; I feel very good."

That day, my husband took an hour nap, the first sound sleep he had in days. When he awoke, he asked for Shinhee again. I told him that she was upstairs and that I would get her later. He smiled and began to talk. "Isn't she beautiful?" he said. "She is perfect." I didn't know who he was talking about at first; this didn't sound like my husband. He never talked about his daughter being perfect. "What?" I asked. "Who are you talking about? Our daughter?" Of course, our daughter, he said. I couldn't believe it. He had always been unhappy with our daughter; they were never close. They disagreed all the time, and although he recognized her many accomplishments, he was never entirely satisfied, or so it seemed. Now he had a change of heart—of course, because he was dying. I knew that, but that wasn't his point. When later I told Shinhee what her father had said, after his funeral, she was freed of her anger about their relationship and his constant dissatisfaction with her, and hers with him. That was my husband's point, I learned. He wasn't trying to make amends for himself before he died; he wanted to leave others with peace.

He did the same with our son. The night before he passed away, our son came in late, around two-thirty in the morning. He had been out with friends all night. When he came in, my husband heard his son and woke up. "Tell him to come here," my husband whispered to me. Our son came into the room and listened to his father.

"You are the number one man in the family; you are responsible now," my husband said.

"Uh-huh," Mike said. He was twenty-five then and still very immature.

"I want you to know that I love you very much," my husband continued. "Remember that: I love you."

Mike continued to nod his head and say, "uh-huh," as my husband repeated his message four or five more times.

My husband felt he shouldn't die on a Sunday because he was a Christian, and just as I believe he held out a few extra days until our daughter came back from New York, I believe that he refused to die on a holy day. If my daughter had come home on Wednesday when he asked for her, I think my husband would have died on Thursday. But she arrived on Saturday, and my husband couldn't die on Sunday, so he held out until Monday. That Sunday he was throwing up blood, so I called the doctor. The hospital told me that I could bring him in or let him stay home, but he was ready to die and there was little they could do for him except make him comfortable. I asked my husband what he wanted to do, and he decided to go to the hospital. We took him in our car rather than an ambulance. I asked the nurse to give him a painkiller, so she administered a shot. An hour later, my husband still was in pain, so I asked for another shot. Do you know what happened? The second shot helped him, but not by easing his pain; he fell into a coma. He never had any pain after that, but I never got to talk to him again. He was asleep forever.

I stayed with him through the night, but I was so tired, I needed to rest my eyes for a while and asked my daughter to keep watch and wake me up if he stirred. Around midnight, I woke up and asked my daughter if he had done anything. She said his condition hadn't changed; he only scratched his nose around eleven o'clock. I listened and noticed that his breathing had become more labored than before, and I had that feeling, so I told Shinhee to take hold of his one hand while I held the other and we prayed for the next hour. All of a sudden, he made a noise. Not until after he died did I realize that he was talking; that was the noise I heard him make.

In those final minutes, shortly after he made that noise, all I could do was pray. I yelled at him: "Hold Jesus' hand tight! You are leaving us now. Just hold His hands!" Over and over, I screamed those words. Then his breathing became labored again, and for a few minutes, his breath seemed only to go out; I imagined feathers flying from his lips. At one-forty in the morning, he died. I don't know if I prayed or cried. None of it seemed real. All I could think was that my final words to him were prayers; I never got to say what I really wanted him to hear. I wanted to tell him that I never really gave him a fair chance. I wanted to tell him I was sorry for all the things I did wrong. I wished I had told him: I love you. It is my forever regret.

Later, I called our pastor's home and announced that my husband had died. My church pastor and all the elder stewards from the church came and prayed. Before my husband died, he had made his funeral arrangements with a church elder. He had picked out his burial plot from a map of the church cemetery that a friend brought. He called up his old friend and asked him to sing at his funeral. However, his poor friend thought my husband had gone too far with his joke, as he hadn't heard that my husband was even sick.

At the funeral, he sang Hymn Forty: "How Great Thou Art." Many people came to pay their respects to my husband. Several young people said they hoped to be as happy and peaceful in their final days as my husband was in his. I agreed, but I also knew that my husband was not always a happy person. He didn't have a happy younger life. A war orphan, he struggled early and because of all that he suffered, he grew up with a lot of anger and unhappiness inside. Oh, he could be so much fun and so attractive at times, but inside, he always seemed so angry and bitter. But in his final two months, he changed. He became an angel. I barely recognized him as the man I had married.

I have always thanked God for that, my husband's final transformation. Even though my husband never really prayed, read the Bible or attended church regularly, there were others who prayed for him. Our best friends, my siblings, especially my sister in Los Angeles, all my family members, my church members, and me. We all prayed very hard for two continuous years for his salvation, and in his final days, we were answered.

The day we got news of his terminal cancer, I stopped praying. Do you know what my pastor told us? He said that praying is like a bank; you can save up prayers. I guess I had enough in savings.

My husband was fifty-nine when he died, just two months from his sixtieth birthday. I was fifty-six. A few years later, our son announced that I would be a grandmother soon. His girlfriend was pregnant. They didn't have enough money to pay for a wedding, so I prepared one for them. Mike was married in September 1998, and our first grandchild, a baby girl, was born in December. I became a grandmother around my sixtieth birthday.

And last year, my son and his wife had their second child, so now I have a grandson. My husband would be proud.

God is very good to me. My husband is gone, but I have grandchildren.

Searches

*I*n 1986, CHSM launched its first Korea tour group. We had fewer than thirty people in our group. The next year, there were a few more. The Olympics were in Seoul in 1988, so we took a year off, and in 1989, the tours became part of our post-adoption services. Since then, we've gotten bigger and bigger and better and better.

Over the years, I have helped many adoptees find their birth families and unraveled many sad stories. Mostly, I translated for the adoptees and their birth families, and most times I cried with them. Still, I believed in adoption. I knew that adoption wasn't perfect or the best solution, but I believe adoption is good for the child, for the birth parents, and for the adoptive parents, and it is much better than letting children grow up in orphanages in Korea. I believe the United States is the best country for international adoption, as it is a melting pot; there is better opportunity here, even if many children grow up in largely white communities. Besides, our world is not going to be so white in the future; white is not going to be in the majority forever.

Orphaned children in Korea couldn't go to school back in the early days of adoption, and certainly not college. Korean parents spend so much money on their children's education, and that's just through high school. College is something else. That's why so many Korean parents now send their children to America for college. There is more opportunity here and entrance into college is not as expensive or competitive as it is in Korea. If a student does not do well on the college entrance exam, she cannot get into a good college, and that means she cannot get a good job. Korea has more limitations than America. That's why I believe in adoption. I do understand how difficult it is to grow up as a minority here; my own children have taught me that. But I also know that my children have had more opportunities than they would have had in Korea.

Even if a child were to stay in Korea with the birth mother, but the father abandoned them, that child and mother would live in misery. There are many types of families in America that are accepted. In Korea, there is only one kind of family and that is a mother and father and child. A child without a mother or a father or both would be ridiculed. A child with only one parent or no parents would not be considered a good candidate to get married in Korea. Family background and bloodlines are too important.

My son, Mike, is adopted. If we had stayed in Korea, he would have had a very difficult life, even though he was adopted by a Korean family. In Korean minds, he would still be considered an orphan. As long as an adoptee has a strong inner self, she can be anything she wants in America. That is not the case in Korea. Adoption is a great opportunity for children who need families.

People ask me if I ever want to return to Korea. I was born there; I grew up there. I speak the language and know the culture, unlike many adoptees. Do you know what my answer is? No. I live here now; I am a Korean-American. Korea is a different country to me now. Whenever I visit, by the end of my trip, I am ready to come back home. To America. This is the place I call home now. I was thirty-seven when I left, so I remember it well. Now I'm sixty-four, almost sixty-five, and I don't recognize the place where I grew up. The Korea I knew doesn't exist anymore, just as I think that the Korea that adoptees dream about doesn't exist. It's similar to how they think their life might have been better had they grown up with other Koreans; they think it would have been easier than growing up in America.

Three brothers

Three brothers were separated as children. When they were school age and toddlers, the oldest one stayed in Korea while the two younger ones were adopted to America. The adopted brothers were about 19 and 25 when I helped them search for their oldest brother and their birth mother. One of them remembered the oldest brother and the village where they lived because he was adopted when he was older. They asked CHSM about doing this search, but the Korean agency replied that they couldn't locate the birth family.

The young man persisted and asked if we would just help him find the area where he used to live. We arranged an afternoon trip with a Korean tour guide. Fifteen minutes after they arrived, the older brother was found. You see, the agency had just sent a letter before, and the letter was returned as undeliverable. But because the search used only a letter and not a person who could visit the area, no one realized that the family was still there, just not at the same address.

The brothers were reunited and very happy, but later I heard that there were problems. One of the younger American brothers had a job and worked hard but his oldest brother in Korea was lazy and needed financial help. Assuming that his younger brother was a rich American, the older brother asked his American sibling for money repeatedly. Finally, the adoptive parents came to the office with their two sons, and told us the story. I was very upset. That family didn't know that this was not the Korean way, and the younger brother didn't understand that he was not obligated to give his oldest brother money. In this case, the older brother was just lazy and wanted to live off of his new-found American sibling. The older brother made the younger one feel as if it was his duty as a Korean because the younger brother got a good education in America and had more opportunities.

This was wrong. No Korean family should expect such a thing from the child who was adopted to America. That creates dependency, and that is not good for either side.

A mother's story

I translated between a Korean birth mother and the daughter she had placed for adoption many years ago. When we arrived at the hotel to meet the mother, I saw a woman holding a beautiful flower basket she had made. This woman recognized her daughter based on a picture she saw. The three of us talked for four hours straight that night and had to continue the next day. The daughter understood her birth mother's story. All of us cried so much that night. The mother even offered to help the daughter find her birth father, but the daughter refused. This is why:

Your father was very abusive and an alcoholic. He beat me and kicked me and locked me out of the house many times. Once, he beat me so bad I lost a piece of my ear. See these scars on my face? These are from your father. I was pregnant with you when all this was going on. Your father was working at a construction site, and my responsibility was to prepare his twelve-man crew's meals—three times a day. Every day I shopped for ingredients, then spent the morning, noon and night chopping and cooking by myself. At night, your father came home and drank all night. One night, he beat me and threw me out in the snow. Some neighbors found me, and I ended up giving birth to you in that cold winter snow. I knew that I could not keep you, so I brought you to the adoption agency and then I disappeared. I left your father for good. Later, I heard that your father had married again or was living with another woman but that he continued to search for me. Now, I work as a housemaid part-time and make enough money to support myself, but I am still afraid your father will find me. And if he does, I know he will kill me. Can you understand that I had no choice? If I had kept you, I never would have been able to leave your father and start a new life. I was a slave; I wanted you to be free.

The daughter was crying, reassuring her Korean mother: "I love you, I love you, I do not hate you because you sent me for adoption." She said this repeatedly.

Lost, then found

A family of about eight came on the tour one year. The brother and sister were adopted together when they were older, so they remembered the last time they saw their birth mother; she left them at the train station then disappeared. We were able to locate the birth mother. When we met, I saw that she had scars—pock marks—all over her face. Soon, we understood why:

Your father, my husband, was a wonderful man. He was the nicest, kindest person I had ever met. Do you see my face? I had these scars when I met him. To Koreans, my face is very ugly. But your father, he loved my heart. He saw what was inside me, and he asked me to marry him. His mother was against the marriage, though, because she felt I was not good enough for her son, but in the end, we had to marry because I was already pregnant. Because the mother-in-law hated me and said I embarrassed her family with my ugliness, we did not live with her. Your father and I lived happily with our first two children, and then we had two more. Later, your father became ill and died, leaving me with four children to care for. The first two were old enough by then to take care of themselves, but the two younger ones—you two—were still too young to be left home alone while I worked. At that point, I thought I only had two choices: either kill my two youngest children or kill myself. My friend said I had a third choice: adoption. That was when I took you to the train station. I knew someone would find you and bring you to an orphanage, but do not think this was easy for me. After I left you both, the part of me that was part of you died.

Those two children were both happily married, and came to Korea with their adoptive parents. They all cried listening to their Korean mother's story, but I cried as much as the two young people. Later, they kidded me about why I cried so much. But who wouldn't?

True happiness

I remember another large family that came on our Korea tour one year. They were from Nebraska or Iowa. There were six in the family, including a grandmother. The wife wasn't healthy, and they had chosen that year for the trip in case she was unable to travel in the future. Unfortunately, the parents didn't have a lot of money and that trip was their biggest expense. I saw that this family did not buy very many things like the other people on the tour. All the other families bought all kinds of things, and parents gave their children money. Finally, I asked the mother how she and her husband could afford to bring their entire family on such an expensive tour. She explained that they had taken out a second mortgage on their house to pay for the trip. She worried that her health would not allow her to travel if they waited another year or two or ten, and her husband's work was not going well. "This was the year to go," she said. "If we didn't do it now, we would never go. The children are getting older and will leave home soon, so we wanted to do it as a whole family. We're enjoying every single minute."

In fact, the entire family truly did look happy to simply enjoy the trip. They really made an impression on me. The parents were amazing people, and I respect them deeply.

Stones in his pocket

There was one boy, maybe fifteen or sixteen, when he came on our Korea tour. We did a search for him but weren't able to find anything on his background. The place of his birth had changed and now was a bank, so there were no records to be retrieved, no paper trail to follow. This young man still wanted to go to that site, just to see what the area looked like. We pulled up across the street from the bank, and he got out and crossed the street himself. I watched him stand there and then he bent over and picked something up and put it in his pocket. When he came back to the car, his face was wet with tears. Curious, I asked him what he had put in his pocket. From his pocket, he withdrew a few small stones and held out his hand. "This was the place where I was born," he said. That just broke my heart. Those little stones were all he had to link him to his past. I wished I could have found out more for him. All we knew was that his birth mother was young and after giving birth, she could not afford to keep a baby so she left after leaving her baby for adoption. That was all we had and it wasn't enough to find that woman now. Whenever I remember his story, my heart breaks for him.

It's not fair

On the last night of one of our tours, we had a big party and had people share their experiences about the trip. One young man said he had a lot of fun and was glad he was able to come on the tour, but it didn't seem fair that some people found their foster mothers and birth mothers while his search turned up nothing. He was happy for the others, but he said he couldn't help feeling how unfair it all was.

One or two years later, we social workers were invited to his high school senior class speech, at his graduation with hundreds of students. In his speech, he thanked his adoptive parents and credited them for much of his success. I was moved so much, and had a lot of tears throughout his speech. I never would have thought that this young man was the same one who, years before, complained about life not being fair. When I heard him say that on the tour, I was bothered because that's all most people hear. The stories people *don't* hear are about adoptive families that are happy. In fact, the vast majority of adoptees are happy with their adoptive parents, but we seem to hear many negative stories. Believe me, most stories are like this young man's story.

The media

One year, a college student came on our tour group alone. Let's call him Bruce. His adoptive parents chose not to go, and his younger brother—also adopted, also his biological brother—had no desire to search for their birth family. We found out that Bruce was adopted when he was six or seven, and his younger brother was four or five, so Bruce remembered his family life. He remembered that their father abused their mother and that he also had a little sister. And he knew why he and his brother were abandoned.

Because of the abuse, the mother decided to run away with her children. She put the two boys on a city bus first and gave them instructions to their uncle's house. Do not fall asleep, she warned, or you will miss your stop and be lost.

The boys nodded their heads and promised not to fall asleep, but of course, they fell asleep. The bus ride was long and they were sleepy and alone. When they woke up, the bus had reached its final stop and now they were, indeed, lost. At the bus station, they sat and cried. A police officer found them and took them to the nearby orphanage, and not long after, they were adopted.

Bruce was determined to find his mother and sister on our tour. I located his hometown, near Kyoung-ju, where we stayed for three days. We found the orphanage easily and were able to talk to the director who was at the orphanage at the same time as Bruce. The director remembered Bruce even though he was grown and had dyed hair. He said, "I remember you! You had a younger brother and said you knew karate, like tae kwon do." Bruce didn't recognize the director, but he knew the director knew him because he had told the other kids that he knew karate so they wouldn't beat him up. Problem was that his bragging got him in trouble; the other kids challenged him—they wanted proof.

We took a tour of the orphanage, and Bruce remembered that the building we met the director in was not the original orphanage he grew up in, and he was right. We went inside an older building and suddenly, Bruce had his bearings. "There was a ramen shop here," he said. Despite all the changes in the area, he recognized and remembered a lot.

Earlier, I had asked Bruce for some more clues to the area he grew up in. He remembered a big bear outside of a church, a small drinking house nearby and that his father wore a tie to work and drove a small truck. I had also asked a friend at another agency to help us by contacting the television station. Sometimes we used the media to help us search, and in this case I felt that was our best chance. The four-person TV crew came with us to Kyoung-ju and paid for everything; they also had done some searching on their own, wanting to ensure a successful story for themselves as well. A key piece of information they discovered was of a village leader's meeting that was taking place during our visit. The older villagers would be attending and someone might know something about Bruce's family, we thought.

Excited, we went to the meeting and asked the village chiefs. No one knew of Bruce's family or their names; they told us that the village had grown and been rebuilt since Bruce was a child. Unwilling to give up, I thought of a clue Bruce had given me. I asked the villagers if any of the areas had a seventeen-year-old or older church. The answer was yes. We went to that area and saw that it had been developed recently, so Bruce didn't recognize any of it, but when we went to see the church, Bruce remembered the bell stand in front—even without the bell. I asked some people if they remembered a drinking house in the area many years ago, and they said yes. In the end, we found out that the mother ran away with the baby girl and shortly after, the father left town as well because the house was not his; they rented a room, and when they left, no one paid attention to them.

At this point we didn't have a next step, so I suggested that we visit the district office and search for records of any young boys from that area who never showed up for the draft. You see, military duty is mandatory in Korea, and the government keeps track of those young men who don't report for duty. Bruce and his brother were now over age twenty-one and would've shown up in government records as draft dodgers. Once in a while, I surprised myself that I could have such a good idea! We then found the mother's name and father's name—even the mother's phone number. Unfortunately, the father had passed away by then, about seven or eight years before. After these discoveries, the TV crew decided we should take a break and go eat lunch, as we hadn't eaten all day.

Bruce wanted to contact his mother, of course, but the TV crew took over the search. They said he had to have his mother come to the TV station so that the reunion could be aired. You see, they still had a show to do and felt that they had the right to make demands because they had played a key role in the search. I knew I couldn't have done it without their help. They saved us time and got us important information. So after lunch, they called the mother and, after they confirmed that the lady's name was the same as on the records, they gave me the phone right away. She had a husky voice, and wondered who the man was, and who was this "Mrs. Han" she was now talking to. I introduced myself and informed her that her son was standing by my side now. She stopped breathing for a moment, then hurried to say "I don't believe it." She wanted proof. "My son has a big scar between his eyebrows," she said. "He got it from his father when a can that was intended for me struck my son instead and cut him between his eyebrows." The TV crew confirmed Bruce's scar. His mother began to cry. She asked where we were, as she intended to come right away.

The television people were listening to the conversation, and then took the phone away from me. The crew told Bruce's mother that she had to meet them at the station in order to meet her son. She refused, and they threatened. I know that was cruel, but they wanted to do their show; that's how it was. When the television crew insisted that this was

the only way they would let her meet her son, the mother
hung up. She ended up coming to the station but held a
handkerchief in front of her face so no one would recognize
her when the show aired. Later, I told Bruce that he could
come back to the hotel with his mother and I would translate
for them. She showed up at the hotel with her daughter—
Bruce's little sister—and her husband's sister and her four
grown children, and she shared her story:

*Son, I was more than ten years younger than your father. I
was very pretty then. Your father drank a lot and he beat me. I
had to escape.*

*I never remarried, and now I run a small restaurant. But
you know, my life was never my life, not after I put my two
little boys on that bus alone and they were lost to me forever. I
felt so guilty; I never should have let you boys go alone. You were
too young. Everyone blamed me for a long time and accused me
of abandoning my children. No one believed my story; they
thought that if it was true, you boys would have found your
way home eventually. For a long time I lived with that guilt.
Now I can tell my family that I was not lying. Now they will
believe that I never meant to abandon my boys. And now I can
forgive them for blaming me all these years. I hope you can
forgive me.*

That evening, Bruce knocked on my hotel door and
presented me with a necklace he had bought earlier. I knew
it was for his girlfriend back home and told him to bring it
back home and give it to her. He said no and insisted that he
would give her something else. It could have been the first
and last precious gift I received from a young adopted
person. I think, eventually, his entire adoptive family—
including his younger brother—returned to Korea to meet
the birth family.

The twins

A few years ago we had a mother and daughter who came to Korea while we were there with a tour group. The girl was about nineteen; let's call her Julie. We had done a search already and found the girl's birth family, as well as all the details surrounding her adoption story. What Julie was told was that she was adopted because her birth mother couldn't raise her, and that she had a brother in Korea who was believed to be her twin. But we knew he wasn't. And the alleged twin brother didn't know either.

Julie's birth family knew that we were coming, and they had told their son—her "twin" brother—that he was going to meet his long-lost twin sister who had been adopted to America.

You see, in Korea, a husband and wife often lived with the husband's parents. If the couple did not eventually produce a son to continue the family name, the mother-in-law sometimes kicked her daughter-in-law out of the house. Julie's mother had four daughters and was pregnant again. Afraid that this was her last chance to have a son, she panicked when she gave birth to a fifth girl: Julie. Somehow, the mother knew that a baby boy had been born the same day and was going to be placed for adoption. So she arranged to switch the children; she would give up her daughter for adoption and take the baby boy. Then she went home and told everyone she had a baby boy.

When the Korean social worker called her and told her who she was, Julie's birth mother nearly fainted, of course. Fortunately, she had told her husband the truth about a year after the switch. He was angry with her at the time and from then on, he felt he could not trust her. He was not bitter, but almost half-joking about it. Their four daughters had all heard the story from their mother, and they were very sympathetic. When we called, she told her husband about our impending visit and the husband said, of course, his daughter could come and meet them. The problem was explaining this long-lost daughter to their son, so they decided to make up a story. They told the son that many years ago, his mother had given birth to twins—the son and Julie—but they already had four daughters. Also, they told their son, we were very poor at the time and could not afford two more children so we decided to give up Julie for adoption. Now she lives in America and has found us and wants to meet us, they said.

I went to the airport with Jeff Mondloh, the Post-Adoption Services director of the Korean Program. While we were waiting there for the mother and daughter to arrive from Minnesota, we met the four sisters. They were so excited to talk about their sister, how she looked, how pretty she was, and so forth. I asked them if they could truly be a sister to Julie, and they all answered "Yes!"

The family met—including the "twin" brother—and everyone agreed to keep the truth secret. After that incident, I wondered how many more stories there were out there like that, and I knew this was a story that could not be told in Korea. At least not for a while. Otherwise, Korean husbands whose wives had given birth to opposite-sex twins would wonder if that was the truth or deception. I don't know if this happens as much anymore, but Koreans' long preference for boys over girls has resulted in some rather unusual—and sad—stories.

Unspoken identities

About three or four years ago there was a young girl about twelve or thirteen years old who wanted to search for her birth family. I'll call her Amanda. She came on our tour and we visited the hospital in which she was born. We were able to get a record of her birth. My friend who was retired from high up in the government had come with us and asked the hospital if the records showed any identifying information about the birth mother or father. The hospital staff said yes, there was a name and address, but they couldn't release the information. Understanding Korean ways, I did not put up a fuss and left quietly. Meanwhile, my friend secured the information.

We discovered that Amanda's family was still living in the area but it was in a part of the countryside where there were no phones. That's all we were able to do during the tour. After we returned to the States, I asked my friend to visit the family and take a picture of the mother and send it to me. I had left her a picture of the daughter and some information.

My friend didn't go right away. She didn't know what to do. She couldn't just show up and take this woman's picture without revealing her purpose. Finally, she came up with a plan. She got her sister to donate a few hundred dollars to her department and say that it was to be used to help that poor country family. My friend took one of the ladies from the local government office with her and the two of them, driven by my friend's husband, went to give this family the "donation." They arrived at a very poor farmhouse. The husband wasn't home. Only the wife (birth mother) was there with a little child; she told my friend's party that her other two children were in school. The government staff person explained that they were there on government business. According to a report, the staff person said, their office had gotten word that this family worked very hard but still needed some financial support. The wife said they didn't need total support but a little extra help would be nice. She went on to explain how poor they were and how much money they made each year. The staff person said the government would provide financial support to the family for one year, but they needed to take a picture of the family members for their files. So that is how we got this mother's picture—and the little girl who was home with her.

When I saw that picture I couldn't believe how much Amanda's face resembled her birth mother's; they had exactly the same face. The problem, though, was that my friend could not tell this family about the adopted daughter who was looking for them. My friend explained that this mother had signed the relinquishment papers many years ago, and that meant she had no legal rights over her adopted child. That also meant that it was illegal for the government to intervene and tell her about her daughter, Amanda; the relinquishment papers stated as much back then. We couldn't interfere or upset the mother's current situation.

On the American side, Amanda and her adoptive parents didn't understand the secrecy and withholding of information. They pushed me again last year to try and convince my friend to change her mind. I tried to explain to both sides the difficulty of the situation. You see, we weren't trying to withhold information; Koreans don't deliberately lie to adoptees. This is the Koreans' way of protecting the adoptee, hard as that is for adoptees to understand. Koreans think that adoptees should put the past behind them and not dig up what might be ugly stories. What good will it do? Koreans think. The past does not change the future, they say.

Now that I am retiring, I am not sure what will happen with Amanda and her situation. I want to help her but I don't know how. The solution is not so easy.

Twin girls

Another search took me to Kyoung-sang Province, down south. I went with the twin girls who had been adopted and their adoptive parents to visit the place of their birth. When they were born, the place was used by a midwife, but when we arrived we found a meat shop in its place.

We found out that the owner of the meat shop was the midwife's son, and that his mother was still living and she was home. Behind the shop was their house, so the old lady came out to greet us. She was probably close to eighty years old. She invited us into a small room and said that it used to be the waiting area; the delivery room was now part of the meat shop, she said. I told her about the twins' case and she remembered delivering them. She explained:

Few people delivered twins then. Also, I remember that your birth mother had a strange delivery; she lost a lot of blood and had to be taken to the hospital for a blood transfusion. I don't recall every detail about your mother but I think she might have been married because she wasn't a young girl. Your mother was bleeding too much for me to waste time getting a lot of information; she needed to get to the hospital. She only told me that she was married and came from a poor area. When she saw that she had delivered twin girls, she said she wanted to give them up for adoption. That was the best decision at the time, you know. She was too poor to care for two girls.

We took a picture of those twin girls sitting next to the midwife in front of the meat shop. That was to be their search story. You see, sometimes we found the birth family and other times we could not. Back then, records were not kept because no one ever imagined that these children would return years later as adults to search for their birth families.

Unearthing secrets

Kim was fourteen or fifteen when we helped her with her search. We knew that Kim had been raised in the southern part of Korea by someone she called "Auntie," until she was placed for adoption at age four. We also discovered that this "Auntie" was really Kim's mother all along.

We were able to locate Kim's birth mother in Korea and called her up. The mother refused to see her daughter. She had remarried and now had a baby boy; her current husband didn't know about her daughter, Kim. I pushed, though, and based on what this woman said about her current husband, I felt sure that she could tell her husband without ruining their present life. Finally, she agreed to meet.

Last summer, I went with Kim to meet her birth mother. The mother traveled three hours to meet us. She was a very pretty woman and looked like she still was in her twenties, which was about the age she was when she gave up Kim for adoption. Funny thing, the daughter wasn't as pretty as her mother; Kim took after her father. The mother explained that her husband was away in the army, but she had told him about this meeting. He loved her so much, she said, that he was not upset or angry with her about her past. In the end, Kim was able to meet her grandmother and extended family.

First and last encounter

A thirteen-year-old girl's adoptive parents contacted us and asked to do a search for their daughter's birth mother. They explained that their daughter had not requested the search— yet—but if she ever wanted to know about her birth family, they wanted her to have the information.

We found the girl's birth mother and called her up. At first she thought there was a problem. She said: the agency told me that if I signed over my rights, they would keep everything confidential; that was the agreement, right? When I explained that we had her daughter's information and could arrange a meeting, the woman was shocked. She refused and explained that she had lied to her husband about their daughter and told him the baby girl had died. No way will I see my daughter or contact her, she said.

I asked a local social worker to keep tabs on the case and keep me updated. Over the next six years, the woman moved several times and changed her phone numbers constantly. But we always found her. Meanwhile, the daughter was growing up and decided she wanted to find her birth mother. The social worker who was helping me went to the woman's house and waited for her on her doorstep. When the woman came home, the social worker told her that her daughter wanted to meet her. The mother said, "Are you crazy?" Still, she refused. I talked to her on the phone again and pleaded once again. I asked her to just meet me and I would try to help her and figure something out.

She was a beautiful lady in her forties when we met. She said her husband's business was very successful, and if he ever found out that she had lied, he would kill her. This is final, she said; don't ever tell me again that my child wants to see me. I persisted, though, and said she had to meet her daughter at least once. Just once. That was two years ago. Last year, the girl's adoptive mother called me and said her daughter was getting ready for college and wanted to try to contact her birth mother once more.

I contacted a social worker in Korea, who found the birth mother again and finally, the mother agreed to meet— under one condition: that we never request another meeting ever again. The adoptive mother and daughter met the birth mother and were very happy but wish they could keep in touch with the birth mother. Unfortunately, that is out of my control. The birth mother kept her part of the bargain; we have to keep ours.

Korean adoptions have changed since I started as a social worker. When I first came in 1975, we never kept in touch with the adopting parents because we believed that they could raise the children just fine themselves. The most important thing was to find the children a home. As the years passed, agencies shifted their services to meet the changing needs of adoptive families. We developed so many more resources, like post-adoption, to provide support and resources for families beyond the actual adoption process. But nowadays, I see adoptive parents who are far more independent. They don't seem to need agency resources as much, maybe because there are so many other resources out there and so much information on the Internet.

Now the first generation of adoptees has grown and become adults and some of them are speaking out against adoptions. There is a young man from Sweden who is lobbying the Korean Congress to stop overseas adoptions. He believes adoption is bad, yet I look at him and think he has reaped only the benefits of adoption. He has a doctorate but he wants to prevent all those children in orphanages from the same chance at such an education?

Since the year 2000, I understand that the number of children in Korean orphanages continues to rise. This is very sad. I wonder if that Swedish adoptee understands the extreme discrimination that an orphan faces in Korea, or even the discrimination a child adopted in Korea faces. I wish young people who think adoption is not good because they had bad experiences while growing up, would understand the reality of life in Korea as an orphan or adoptee. Yes, I know that it is difficult to grow up in non-Korean places, but stopping adoptions is not the answer.

Do you realize that we are in danger of coming full circle? In the 1940s there were orphanages all over America. They eventually closed them down and started adoption and foster care programs, and now look at us: there are those who want to open those institutions back up. I'm not happy about that. There is an orphanage that someone is trying to build right now in Minnesota. The Koreans will laugh at us and say: *See? You build orphanages, too!*

Looking
Back
Looking
Ahead

Now that I am retired and, I hope, a bit older and wiser, I can talk about some of my successes and failures over the span of my life and career.

My greatest strength has also been my greatest weakness: I am strong-willed. Sometimes, that stubbornness has come across as a bluntness that I don't intend. Other times, I must admit that I truly did intend to be blunt, or to have my way, because I believed in what I was doing.

I have a very large forehead. In Korea, we say that people with large foreheads have very big hearts; those people are very generous, loving, caring and giving. So do you know what I did? I tried to live up to my forehead and become that kind of person from a very young age. I wasn't very attractive-looking as a child, but I thought I was something special because of my large forehead. That was my identity. Even my school friends said so. One of my friends from Ewha University said to me, "Even though my eyesight is not very good at long distances, I can see your forehead coming at me like a giant playground." It was my duty, I thought, to be what people expected, and they expected me to be generous and forgiving. When I felt hurt or angry, I kept it inside, or tried to forgive and forget as soon as possible. I believed that people would not approve of any angry behavior if I was supposed to be such a warm and caring person.

I have been very blessed in my life. Because of my parents, I grew up feeling unique and special. I believe that all people are unique and special, but many children grow up never knowing or hearing that message. I think my parents gave me my strong identity and self-esteem. Somehow, I always knew that I would make something of myself and do something important. I wish all children would grow up knowing their potential, and that they would learn that from their families.

Being a Christian gave me self-confidence. Remember how I came to the church originally? To cure my speech problem? Well, over the years, the church taught me that I was special because I was God's child. I also learned that God gave each of us unique talents that we were to make use of. My worry was that God blessed me with many talents and I have not been able to use them all. Or perhaps I felt that I had all these wonderful gifts and didn't know how to use them. I feel this pressure even now that I am older, especially now that I am retiring.

Everyone asks me what I will do after retiring. My passion for the past forty years has been centered on adoption for children who need families, especially Korean adoption. But just as I explained about my high school and college years, once I leave a phase in life, I don't look back. I know I have given that part of my life more than one hundred percent. Of course, looking back on my years as a social worker I sometimes think 120 percent wasn't enough; I wish I could have given 150 percent, or more. But I am only human; the rest I leave in God's hands.

It is now time to find new passions. These new passions will be my other talents that I must develop and use. I look forward to my next one, which will involve my church and mission work. I hope I am able to do those things, depending on my health and the opportunities that I might get. That is what I've been praying to God for during the past few years, and I am sure He will answer sometime, in some way. And if I can't do that, that may also be His answer.

When I think back on my life, I realize that I was blessed with the most important things: family, work, education, faith. Some people who know me may be surprised that I feel this way, as I sum up all the good things that have come to me.

Through the years they might have heard me say that I didn't have many possessions, or an important title, or a high-paying job. At times, I might have been upset with my husband, or disappointed in my children, or concerned that my social class was no higher than when I began. By some standards, I suppose this could be partially true. If I ever complained, that might be my strong will and bluntness talking.

But in my heart, and through Christian eyes, I consider myself most blessed. I have had enough money for what I needed, I have a title that people recognize, I had a career that made a difference to people's lives. I had a real marriage with both good and bad, and my children became their own individuals with minds of their own. And they gave me my grandchildren! My social class includes my closest friends.

I have so many wonderful people in my life, and I worked with such a great agency. My friends, my families, my co-workers and supervisors: they are all so personable and supportive and still seem to love me dearly even after I've retired. This means so much to me, and I love them all. And I love my daily life because of all these people.

And that was my success, that I knew so many people and families. Without those adoptive parents our children could not have had such a good and loving life here. Not all adoptions turn out to have happy endings, and a few had troubles along the way. I was deeply involved in some of those difficult situations. But so many of those children who had a tough time are now good mothers and good fathers. The Korean government is always asking me for big success stories: did an adoptee became a famous Congressman or a lawyer or a doctor? I'm not concerned if they grow up to be famous or to have a prestigious job. I want them to be good parents, or to have rewarding careers, and to be good sons and daughters to their own parents. That's my real success, and my real pride. If a parent says to me: "We have a good daughter. We are so proud of her," then I feel that I have truly been a success. I return all my success to God, because He helped me. God was involved in my life from the very beginning, right up to now, and He will be until I go to Him.

So if those families want to send me their annual Christmas cards, I hope they will. If they want some prayer requests, I will gladly do that. If they invite me to their children's weddings and graduations, I cannot go to all the events, but I will keep them in my heart at their special times. Even their sad times, like a short while ago, when I lost one of my placement children, a son, only 26 years old, from a traffic accident. That was a tragedy instead of a happy time, but I still could share my comfort and my prayers with his family. Your families are your whole life, but sometimes I feel like they are my life, too.

Earlier in my book, I told how the President of Ewha University, Dr. Ok Gil Kim, taught me an important lesson in how to live my life. She asked that I always do three things. Her lesson came from the Bible: Thessalonians 1, Chapter 5, Verses 16–18. Let me pass them on to you:

Rejoice evermore;
Pray without ceasing;
In every thing give thanks.

I rejoice in all of you, I pray for you, and I thank you all for being part of my life, and for letting me be a part of yours. With love and God's blessings,

Hyun Sook Han
April, 2004

The "Mrs. Han's Retirement Event" could never have happened if there had not been two phone calls made to Children's Home Society & Family Services in October 2002, from Mr. Lance Novak, an adoptive father, and Mrs. Cheryl Heley, an adoptive mother. Agency representatives and distinguished Steering Committee members started meeting soon after.

Mr. Brian Boyd, an expert in making many books related to Korean adoption, suggested that I write this book as part of these events. The idea was a shock to me at first, and seemed like an impossible task. I did not feel deserving, first of all, being a small person who has worked hard throughout life, spending 40 years in adoption, and secondly, I did not feel I was a good writer at all.

The Book Committee arranged for Kari Ruth, a brilliant young American Korean adopted person, to interview me, and to write a first draft of the book based on our conversations. Another wonderful young Korean adoptee who is an artist, Kim Dalros, worked on the design of the book for many long hours, and has made it beautiful on the inside and on the cover. Cheryl Heley also sat down to interview me for an additional part of the book. Mrs. Lynne Hessler typed as fast as she could. Mrs. Mary Kay Fitzgerald couldn't have been more helpful as the liaison between all these people and myself.

I can't thank all these people enough.

Very special thanks go to Madonna King, President of Children's Home Society & Family Services, and to David

ACKNOWLEDGMENTS

Pilgrim, Vice President of the Adoption Division, who have been most supportive and have also worked directly on the book.

Finally, I give eternal thanks to my parents, to my late husband, Young U Han, and to my two dear children, Shinhee and Shin Up. I also want to thank the Rev. Kwang Tae Kim, from the Korean United Methodist Church, who helped me to refine my real "identity."

Hyun Sook Han

The friends of Hyun Sook Han are pleased to honor her life of devotion to children by contributing to the Young U and Hyun Sook Han Endowment. All proceeds from the sale of this book will be added to the Endowment.

In 1995, at the death of her husband Young U, Mrs. Han asked that memorials to his life be placed in a permanent fund to generate resources for services to children as offered through Children's Home Society & Family Services. The Young U and Hyun Sook Han Endowment was established for just this purpose and will continue in perpetuity.

When Mrs. Han made the decision to retire, her friends saw this moment as an opportunity to strengthen this family name endowment and perpetuate the values so characteristic of her deep commitment.

Readers of her story are invited to join in contributing to the Endowment. Gifts may be sent to Children's Home Society & Family Services, 1605 Eustis Street, St. Paul, MN, 55108. Donations may also be made through credit card gifts by calling 651-646-7771 or on line at www.chsm.com.

Personal History

Hyun Sook Han
Date of Birth: June 15, 1938
Birthplace: Seoul, Korea

School and Training:

1958 to 1962	B.A. in Social Work, Ewha Women's University, Seoul, Korea
April 1971 to Sept. 1971	Twin City International Programs for Youth Leaders and Social Workers

Employment:

1964 to 1966	Social Worker, International Social Service, Seoul, Korea • Counseled birth parents • Supervised foster homes • Wrote child studies • Handled intercountry adoption
1967 to 1971	Assistant to Program Director, Christian Adoption Program of Korea In-country Adoption Program, Social Work Supervisor
1972 to 1974	Director, Christian Adoption Program of Korea
Jan. 1975 to June 1975	Vice President, Holt Children's Services, Seoul, Korea
July 1975 to 1993	Social Worker, Children's Home Society of Minnesota
Sept. 1993 to Dec. 2003	International Adoption Consultant and Direct Service Social Worker of Adoption and Post-Adoption Services Departments, Children's Home Society & Family Services

Awards:

May 1973	Outstanding Leader, Social Service, from the Minister, The Ministry of Health and Social Services
1986	Outstanding Social Service Award by Korean Elder Association
May 1987	Civil Merit Award from the President of Korea
May 7, 1989	Proclamation of "Hyun Sook Han Day," May 7th, by Rudy Perpich, Governor of the State of Minnesota
Feb. 27, 1991	Mrs. Han was one of five social workers throughout North America to receive this award. She was the winner for the Midwestern Region, which has the largest number of social service agencies.
1993	Elected as an Outstanding Woman Leader by the Governor of Minnesota.
April 1993	Fifth Social Service Awards by Korea Central Daily Newspaper of Minnesota
July 27, 2002	Tribute by KAAN Conference – (Korean-American Adoptee/Adoptive Family Network)
August 9, 2003	Friend of Children Award from NACAC (North American Council on Adoptable Children)

Presentations:

1. *NACAC, AFA, CWLA Presenter at numerous conferences, seminars, and workshops*

2. *Main speaker for groups of Korean adoptive parents, as well as to the staffs and parents of adoption agencies throughout the United States.*

Programs Created:

Korea Day	1975 – Present. Presented over 130 one-day workshops for all adoptive families of Korean children.
Korean Teen Group	1975 – Present. Group activities for Korean-born teenagers.
Korean Pre-Teen Group	1985 – Present. Korean-born pre-teenagers and parents group meetings.
Korean Benefit Dinner for Children in Korea	Started in 1978 – Present. First year raised $3,000; last 3 years raised about $60,000. Now mostly adoptive parents and volunteer group run it.
Korean Children's Day	1982 – Present. Fun children's activities (contents of Korean cultural and traditions) and educational panel discussion for adoptive parents, with Korean festivities and food.
Korean Family Tour	Pioneered by Development Director Jeff Mondloh. Mrs. Han helped with the tour programs and made improvements every year. Tour has been held in 1987, 1989, 1991, and 1993 to the present.

Other Activities:

Since moving to America, Mrs. Han has worked to stimulate Korean government officers, social workers, and Korean news media to be interested in visiting homes of adoptive families in Minnesota, to advocate for a positive picture of international adoption of Korean children in America to Korean society. These efforts have involved:

1. Social Workers, Administrators of agencies in Korea.
2. Government officers for Child and Family Welfare

Services, in local or federal Korean government.
3. Orphanage Staffs.
4. TV, Newspapers, Women's magazines, writers and reporters.

May 1989: MBC TV program, "Adopted Children," helped by Eastern Child Welfare Society and Children's Home Society of Minnesota.

May 1994: KBS (Korean Broadcasting System) came with representatives from Eastern Child Welfare Society to Children's Home Society of Minnesota. Developed excellent and positive program for intercountry adoption, which greatly affected the Korean Government's decision to continue intercountry adoption.

Every year, 30–70 guests from Korea visit CHSM; Mrs. Han has planned and led all activities to give a positive image of international adoption of Korean children.

Publications:

1979   *Growing up in Korea.* Helped picture-taking in Korea and narration with Dr. and Mrs. Spencer.

1980   *Understanding My Child's Korean Origin*, with help of Mrs. Marietta Spencer.
Many articles for Korean magazines and newspapers; number of TV presentations in Korea; newspaper interview in Korea.

Research:

1969   Abandoned Children's Background in Seoul, Korea. As a result, started "Unwed Mother's Counseling" as the first agency in Korea.

1991 to Present   Korean Adopted Young Adult Research, with Mrs. Marietta Spencer.